GIS in the Classroom

Using Geographic Information Systems in Social Studies and Environmental Science

Marsha Alibrandi

Foreword by Charlie Fitzpatrick

HEINEMANN
Portsmouth, NH

Heinemann
A division of Reed Elsevier Inc.
361 Hanover Street
Portsmouth, NH 03801–3912
www.heinemann.com

Offices and agents throughout the world

Library of Congress Cataloging-in-Publication Data
Alibrandi, Marsha.
      GIS in the classroom : using geographic information systems in social studies and environmental
   science / Marsha Alibrandi ; foreword by Charlie Fitzpatrick.
         p. cm.
   Includes bibliographical references.
   ISBN 0-325-00479-X (alk. paper)
   1. Social sciences—Study and teaching—United States—Computer
network resources.   2. Environmental sciences—Study and
teaching—United States—Computer network resources.   3. Geographic
information systems.   I. Title.

LB1584.7 .A45 2003
300'.285'467—dc21   2002152324

Editor: Danny Miller
Production: Vicki Kasabian
Cover design: Judy Arisman
Cover coordinator: Renée Le Verrier
Typesetter: Argosy
Manufacturing: Steve Bernier

Printed in the United States of America on acid-free paper
07 06 05 04 03 VP 1 2 3 4 5

To the memories of

Corinne Williams Alibrandi
Artist, mother, and intensely practical woman, whose words
"love is geography" must have sunk in! Like most mothers, she knew
this book would happen before I did,

and

C. Frederick Alibrandi,
WWII Navy veteran, CEO, and devoted family man.

Also to two friends,
Joe Ferguson and Ann Judge,
whose legendary spirits and work in geographic education
took them all over the world with teachers and students and,
in the end, on September 11, 2001.

Contents

Foreword

In the movie *Ferris Bueller's Day Off,* the social studies classroom scene is a gem. Standing before class, the teacher, in his most soporific voice, "engages" the group through an endless string of "fill-in-the-blank" statements. The search for parroted facts (". . . this would—anyone? raise or lower? anyone? anyone?—raise . . .") goes unrewarded, despite ever simpler items. One by one, the students fall into a hypnotic stupor, to be rescued only by the bell. For many educators, this and other classic parodies of the school experience bear too much resemblance to situations we know about. The humor is wasted on us, because we know the tragedy of such classrooms.

After completing my degree in geography, I started working on a teaching certificate, and we moved right away into practicum experiences. I had the fortune to see both ends of the teacher spectrum. My second practicum was in an urban core junior high school. "Social science?" this fifteen-year teacher asked, when I described my program. "We don't do social *science.* We do social *studies.* Anyone who comes to class and can name the presidents gets a B for the year." The class was what my program leader described as "a good nonexample."

Contrast these scenes with what happens in a number of classrooms across North America, where the teachers engage geographic information systems (GIS). The computer is a tool that promotes divergence, and skilled teachers know how to tap this wellspring of possibilities. With something like three-fourths of all data having a locational component, there is no lack of material for exploration. Faced with this double-barreled explosion of opportunities, and the dizzying growth of information, astute teachers in the social sciences are moving away from simple accumulation of facts. Instead, their students explore, question, sift, integrate, analyze, interpret, evaluate, and act. GIS is the tool to make the job manageable.

Along the way, these students build their own conceptual framework with which to connect all the loose bits of information. And what, to the students in *Ferris Bueller,* would be just another random element in the midden of once-exposed facts, instead has a context into which it fits, thereby becoming easier to understand, remember, and use to advantage. Constructing their own knowledge by wrestling with the information and questions, these students learn to treat information scientifically, not just in the chemistry class with beakers and compounds and procedures, but also in the geography, history, and other "social" classes.

Such grappling with data is seldom a clean or simple process. Classes can cover vastly more material when teacher and textbook combine to present information. It is much more swift and simple—expedient—just to tell students that "policies in this community affect lives a hundred miles away." But it is far more powerful to have students look at a map that integrates watersheds, stream flow, population density, land use, and transportation corridors, and have them hypothesize about the relationships, seen and unseen, and then study the data confirming the relationships. It requires almost no effort to present a numeric summary of the U.S. presidential election in 2000, and much more work to break the data down by state and county, overlaying time zone, local demographics, and historical trends. But students can acquire so much more integrated knowledge and transferable skill through exploration of the data than through simple parroting of the one or two "ultimate facts."

This book examines the stories of several teachers and their students. The communities, schools, grade levels, subjects, and teacher backgrounds vary. The common element is that the teachers expect their students to explore actively the world around them, questioning, integrating, analyzing, and evaluating every step of the way. They treat their subject as a science, their class as a lab, their students as investigators charged with making sense of vast volumes of disparate data, needing guidance and coaching more than answers and dictates.

For these teachers, GIS is a "power tool" with which to emphasize their process. GIS is a tool that *enhances* and *facilitates* good instruction; it does not *guarantee* it, nor does it *provide* quality instruction. Just as a Stradivarius, a fine camera, a perfectly balanced fly rod, and the best cookware cannot solve all problems for a poor violinist, photographer, angler, or cook, GIS is a technology that can be employed well or poorly. Teachers and administrators who expect the afternoon arrival of GIS software to transform classes and methods by morning will be sorely disappointed. But GIS *does* make it easier for teachers to engage students actively in learning, and thus perhaps to help them do things differently or more powerfully.

- With GIS, students who helped fit timber wolves with transmitters watched in amazement as GPS points transmitted by satellite showed the wolves traveling far and wide, through forest, farm, and suburb, across bridges, rivers, and highways. What are the implications of these protected creatures traveling so?

- With GIS, students have examined school district attendance zone boundaries, and explored the alternatives when a school is to be opened or closed. What are implications—for the many and the individual—of lines drawn here versus there?

- With GIS, students have explored the school as a part of its community through time, examining the role it played in the lives its students and teachers led. In what ways have community values been reflected in, and in what way have they been changed by, the nature of the school?

- With GIS, students are mapping invasive weeds, exploring their avenues for dispersal, modeling their impact on community resources. After sharing these data with state agencies and teaching other students to do the same, how have opinions about the value of a school and its students changed within the community?

When teachers have access to tools that facilitate such exploration, and students are encouraged to construct their own knowledge, everyone benefits. When teachers—rarely the technical experts—learn new tools alongside the student, the young learners see powerful models of education as a lifelong process. When students engage GIS tools to examine data in one class, then discover the technology works equally well in another class, their skills compound and their knowledge framework grows more integrated. And as students create data and knowledge and present this to the community and the world, the school becomes more a part of its local and global community, instead of remaining an isolated place, apart from it. When teachers combine good practices with good resources, there's no limit to where their students can go.

Charlie Fitzpatrick
K–12 Schools and Libraries Coordinator
Environmental Systems Research Institute

Acknowledgments

I n fall 2001, while working on this book, the attacks of September 11 impacted this project in riveting ways. Two friends with the National Geographic Society's Geography Education program, Joe Ferguson and Ann Judge, were hosting two teachers and six students from Washington, D.C., on a trip to a Sustainable Seas conference in California when their plane was hijacked and hit the Pentagon. Central figures in promoting Geographic Education in the U.S., these two had supported, inspired, and collaborated with a network of perhaps ten to fifteen thousand teachers and students, traveling with them across the U.S., to the Mediterranean, and opening them to a world of exploration and multicultural understanding.

Charlie Fitzpatrick and I were among hundreds who attended the National Geographic Society's memorial to Joe and Ann in Washington a week after the attacks. In some ways, remembering their brilliant lives and work was a comfort. In the aftermath, as we struggled to understand and to reconstruct our commitments to one another as a nation, we tried to find meaning. It dawned on me that I could contribute 1 percent for peace from my profit from the book. It's far too little, but in this age of extreme corporate wealth and extreme poverty, at least it's something—and we are all trying to find something we can do.

The visits to the schools described in the following chapters were made possible through a faculty research grant from North Carolina State University. These visits were a joy; being part of these scenes of activity has been inspirational, and I can only hope that I have captured their essence. Lois Crowe assisted in the transcription of the audiotaped interviews. Those involved in GIS K–12 will recognize the work and words of these pioneering educators who each believe in the power of students to transform their communities for environmental and social health.

These educators and partners, Dave Gorrill, Jaci Barton, Randy Raymond, Freda Brown, Yichuan Xie, Kathryn Keranen, Lance Hill, John Jones, Rex Taylor, John Nicolucci, and those teachers mentioned by name throughout the book, are the kinds of teachers who take risks but trust themselves and their students to solve problems together. This is ultimately the trust we must put into the hands of students in order for them to be prepared to meet future demands and the inevitable problems that will arise in their lifetimes. This, to me, is ultimately the purpose of social studies.

These classrooms are distinctly different from content-based classrooms. Student and teacher roles are different. Students see teachers leading them and learning with them. Social studies educator Seth Kreisberg described this as "power-with." All of these teachers trusted their students to speak with me in interviews about their work with GIS, and I am deeply grateful for that experience and their generosity in the spirit of learning and teaching.

In each of these settings, the software being used was ArcView, from Environmental Systems Research Institute (ESRI). The role of ESRI (in particular, the work of Charlie Fitzpatrick, George Dailey, and Angela Lee, and, at ESRI Canada, Chris North and Erin D'Allessandro) has been central to integrating GIS in schools. There are other softwares mentioned in the book, but ESRI has taken the international lead in GIS K–12, and the network now extends to Europe, Asia, and Australia.

Many thanks go to Dr. Cheryl Mason Bolick, formerly of the University of Virginia, for introducing me to the core group of social studies teacher educators involved in promoting technology in the social studies. Dr. Mason Bolick, a graduate of North Carolina State University, was instrumental in partnering several institutions in federal "PT3" grants that supported the integration of technology in social studies teacher education. These, through our local principal investigators, Dr. John Park and Dr. Hiller Spires, and Mentor-Net outreach coordinator, Dr. Lisa Grable, have helped teachers across North Carolina by developing workshops and online tools for technology integration.

My colleagues on the Delany history project, Dr. Candy Beal and Dr. Anna Wilson, and the five teachers with whom we worked, Ann Thompson, Rita Hagevik, Betty Mackie, Ginny Owens, and Neville Sinclair, their 125 middle school students, and the alumni interviewed co-constructed a most memorable and meaningful learning experience and community project.

Danny Miller, Bill Varner, and the helpful people at Heinemann have encouraged and tolerated the fits and starts of this project with grace.

Special thanks go to Shannon White, developer of many of the CD activities. Shannon, Ann Thompson, Rita Hagevik, and Barbaree Duke have been co-constructors and co-instructors in the GIS in Education course. As co-educators, they've helped to create the new landscapes of learning—the new relationships and pedagogy—that make technology integration possible, bearable, and worth it!

To my family: my brothers and their families, for their support throughout this process, my deepest gratitude. And to my partner, Andy, for support, cheer, and good sense even as he struggles with the unceasing demands of teaching and testing, thank you.

Introduction

Who could have predicted even twenty-five years ago how life at the turn of the twenty-first century would look? As professionals involved in the teaching and interpretation of social studies, we find ourselves, like everyone else, just trying to make sense of—and survive—the phenomena surrounding us.

If the moniker "the Information Age" sticks in historical perspective, how will social studies teachers have responded to the proliferation of information? Will we have adjusted our practices to fit the conditions? Have even those who held out at first come to use word processing and the Internet as regular means toward student learning?

In this book, we try to reframe social studies for the new century to address conditions we see impacting adolescents, communities, and education itself—a modest proposal! In that context, we see an interdisciplinary technology, geographic information systems (GIS), as particularly useful. GIS is used daily in so many aspects of human activity that it will become one of those skill sets as basic as word processing is today. Looking historically at the uptake of computer use in the classroom, this transition is roughly comparable to the status of word processing integration in 1990.

If you've pulled a travel map off of the Internet, you've used a GIS. You entered an address destination and a starting point—two points on a digital map related in a database of street address locations. Your travel map pops up with a little star at your destination point, you print it, and off you go (if you haven't done this yet, go to <www.mapquest.com>). The databased address information relates to the spatial representation through a coordinated geographic information system (GIS) that uses point references, lines, and polygons to represent areas on the ground.

But the power in GIS is its ability to relate huge databases of information—to store, to locate, and, most important, to analyze information with spatial properties. Charlie, Shannon, and I have all taught GIS to both adolescents and adults. We've had adolescents assisting adults in this process. Technology changes the landscape of teaching to be more collaborative, since the knowledge is distributed—teachers have a better sense of what types of questions to ask of the technology and students have greater facility with the buttons, the mouse, and possibly the Internet. If you've used technology in your classroom, you're familiar with this phenomenon. Might as well get used to it—this is one of the changes that will probably stick, given adolescents' developmentally appropriate inquisitiveness (more on that later in our discussion of spatial cognition). For now, let us invite you to take a look into some school projects that have integrated GIS to benefit both education and the community.

◉ The GIS Connection and Companion CD

Interspersed throughout the book, you'll see icons for the GIS Connection (GISC) activities found on the companion CD located in the back sleeve of the book. We've designed these to make the GIS connection into your social studies class a more direct one. GIS educator Charlie Fitzpatrick of Environmental Systems Research Institute (ESRI) developed and donated his Arc-Voyager demonstration version GIS software for schools and libraries. ArcVoyager functions mirror most of the GIS product ArcView with the exception of saving, so once you've played with ArcVoyager and want to use that map again, it must be saved as a Print Screen. The GIS Connection activities will address how to manipulate ArcVoyager. We recommend playing with ArcVoyager for a few months and then suggest you consider the next step to ArcView. We provide steps toward that in the resources section (see Malone, Palmer, Voigt's *Mapping Our World: GIS Lessons for Educators*).

Overview of the Book

Chapter 1, What's GIS Done for Me Lately?, introduces GIS and its current uses. We discuss social studies as a multidiscipline from which various social problems are addressed, offering that GIS is an important analytical tool for problem solving. We discuss the function of schools in communities, how we see that relationship changing, and the necessity of strengthening that relationship for adolescents to become active participants in the community. We discuss the historic setting of the generation "growing up digital" and the social implications and critical perspectives on technology implicit in the National Council for Social Studies' theme "Science, Technology, and Society."

Chapter 2, Is There Any Spatially Intelligent Life on This Planet?, discusses spatial intelligence and cognition as central to learning in social studies. We then present examples of both spatial and temporal representation in GIS and its new uses in historic, archeological, and ecological studies, and touch upon the new field of environmental history as located in the evolution of intellectual history. We introduce ways students can analyze information across the multidiscipline of social studies and focus on the student as active participant in conducting social studies for community problem solving.

Chapter 3, Where Is GIS in Schools and in Social Studies?, highlights GIS integration in social studies classes in selected projects from across the nation. I describe a visit to a high school classroom that seemed to have all of the perfect conditions for integrating GIS to suggest how the changing landscapes of learning can be better utilized when there is actual research to do and to coordinate through GIS and other technologies. I then introduce the schools and communities profiled in chapters 4, 5, 6, 8, and 9 in a preview to getting inside each school. While each of the following chapters has a different focus because of the uniqueness of its project or course, at each site, two teachers, six students, and two community partners were interviewed. The community partner interviews took me from a downtown high-rise in a major Canadian city to an office at the U.S. Geological Survey headquarters to a doorstep in the Midwest, streamside in New England, and to a middle school media center in the Southeast. Student interviews involved students in drawing representations of themselves in their communities, responding to questions, and meeting in moments between classes and sometimes during class.

Teacher interviews ranged from kitchen tables to one school's planetarium (not all that often in use), to conversations in the car with a handheld tape recorder that recorded every seam in the road, to shared office spaces, to borrowed back rooms in school libraries, to telephone interviews in the evening after school. The interviews were compelling, intriguing, moving, commiserating, funny, and utterly rewarding.

The school chapters describe projects that utilized GIS to address community issues. Each of these schools was a site for a case study in learning and teaching with GIS. Each has a related GIS lesson application that describes GIS processes used to solve the problem. Each, it is important to note, had a partner relationship with ESRI through either ESRI/US or ESRI/Canada. ESRI's leadership in developing access and supporting GIS integration in schools has been unparalleled. Their commitment to GIS for everyone has led to the development of central websites, <www.esri.com/k-12> and <www.esricanada.com/>, and activities; the first book on the topic, *GIS in Schools* (Audet and Ludwig 2000); and the International ESRI EdUC, an international educational user's group conference held in San Diego <www.esri.com/educ>. These resources are absolutely essential in integrating GIS in K–12 education.

Chapter 4, The People Must Prove That There Is Water, presents a community service project from coastal New England in which students used

GPS and conducted water quality testing along a source-to-sea river where pollution and reduced flow had impacted local shellfish beds. The school and community—at odds with one another at first—came to find mutual benefit from the collaborative project. Students collected data using GIS to map their findings over a four-year period and reported each year in two events; one was a local River Day event sponsored by their nonprofit organization partner and the other was a statewide conference for students and teachers involved in environmental community service. The GIS Connections are creating databases and GIS themes from historic information.

Chapter 5, Oral History, GIS, and the Web: Putting African American History on the Map, describes an interdisciplinary oral history project in which middle school students interviewed African American adults who had attended their school in its segregated past. From the interviews, teachers and students developed a historic representation of cultural features of pre- and Civil Rights–era parts of their city. In the process, they learned that what is considered "data" is determined by the cultural perspectives of those who gather the data. The GIS Connections are oral histories and GIS, photos and digital archives, and hotlinking photos to maps.

Chapter 6, Building Community and Movin' On Up in Motor City, describes projects that address community needs—school districting, distribution routes for a food bank, and site location problems for childcare facilities. Community capacity building through a central business district organization and partnerships across school, community college, and state college benefited all of the partners. Students felt connected to this major city through their work. The GIS Connections are site selection: where do we locate the next daycare center?

Chapter 7, Interlude for a Critical Perspective: Are We Bridging the Digital Divide?, addresses the social implications of GIS and technology in general. Maps are not truth; maps are representations. It is necessary to maintain this awareness as we use or construct maps. Particularly relevant to GIS is a discussion of *data*—whose data, who is included in the data, how the data are gathered, and building in students' interpretive strategies for questioning data and representations. Finally, a section entitled "Community as Energy" illustrates why students' energies must become integral if communities are to be sustainable—and how GIS can facilitate that.

Chapter 8, Getting Behind the Map: Critical Thinking and Community Service in the Capital Area, describes a senior capstone double course designed for real-world problem solving through integrating technology. Students took a geology and GIS course combination, studying population growth and watershed issues using fieldwork and satellite imagery. With a U.S. Geological Survey GIS partner, students ground truthed satellite image data. They presented their findings at their county complex to a sophisticated audience outside the nation's capital. The GIS Connection is satellite imagery, raster data, and ground truth.

Chapter 9, Problem Solving in Canada, describes the work of coauthors of a GIS workbook developed for students in a geographics class in which students with extensive preparation in geography use GIS to address problems from transportation planning for the Olympics to mapping ethnic neighborhoods. The GIS Connection is on mapping ethnicity.

Chapter 10, Conclusions and Implications, summarizes the unique features and common factors from the school case studies. From the research in these schools, we recap best practices and infrastructural conditions to support GIS integration.

The Resources section is a guide to the burgeoning resources to support GIS in K–12 education, heavy on Internet resources, industries, and agencies that would likely partner with schools.

1

What's GIS Done for Me Lately?

If you watched the TV weather report today, you saw a geographic information system—a GIS. Those digital clouds floating across the screen are reconstituted data. Some of the data coming from satellites is imagery, some of it is digital information, but all of it must be coordinated using a "geocode" or a locational reference in order to be represented in a map.

A GIS can be used to display all kinds of data if it can be associated with a geolocation like a street address or a longitude/latitude/elevation (known as an x/y/z). GIS has been applied to most governmental and industrial problems because they operate in geographic areas. Whether redesigning school districts or determining service areas, agencies and organizations are using spatial information for planning and operations.

Communications industries must plan and design infrastructures and networks, whether they're cable-borne, wireless, or fiber optically delivered. Transportation agencies and industries map both infrastructures and distribution routes using GIS technologies. Global positioning system (GPS) devices now assist drivers in locating themselves in a GIS map to maximize their travel routing. "The world on time" wouldn't be, without GIS in the planning. Most goods produced and purchased are hastened on their way using GIS (see Figure 1–1).

Local, regional, national, international, and even extraterrestrial planning requires mapped information, so most government agencies, from the town on up, use GIS for planning infrastructure, taxation, school districting, water distribution and sewage networks, zoning, emergency planning, conservation, and preservation. Virtually no regional or state planning is done without spatial analysis. These days the tool of choice for that analysis is a GIS.

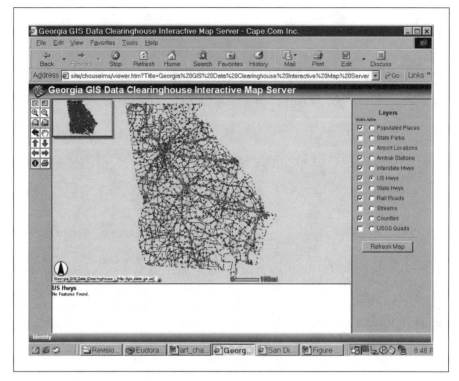

Figure 1–1. *Transportation Map*

Who's Asking Geographic Questions?

In this book, we've combined a general discussion of GIS with case studies of schools that use GIS and activities that might pique your interest in using GIS in a geography or social studies classroom. Central to using GIS, though, is an understanding of *why* one might use it and what types of questions GIS might answer.

What does it mean to ask a geographic question? This is one of the essential elements of geographic education cited by the proponents of geographic education and GIS in education. As social studies teachers in the U.S., most of us are not well prepared in geography. Most are prepared in history, others in political science or the social sciences, a few in economics, but geography? After World War II changed many of the world's maps yet again, geography became the forgotten subject. Perhaps if GIS had been developed back then, changing the maps wouldn't have been so difficult! The result of shifting interests in the postwar era meant a cultural shift away from the global to the immediate, and to retelling history with the U.S. victorious and powerful. Since the 1980s and now, after the terrorist attacks on the World Trade Center and the Pentagon, a new understanding of geopolitics has become both more complex and more necessary.

Meanwhile, the world turns on the same rotations and orbits. In British-style educational systems, geography remains central to the curriculum. Inherited from its former colonial dominance when "the sun never set" on the British empire, the study of geography is alive and well in the U.K., Canada, Australia, and in other former colonies. The French-style curriculum also focused on geography, once essential to all colonial interests.

Since WWII, teachers and students in the U.S. have essentially grown up geographically illiterate. The GENIP group <http://genip.tamu.edu> has clearly demonstrated this gap in U.S. education. (GENIP is the Geographic Education National Implementation Project, composed of constituent members AAG (American Association of Geographers), AGS (American Geographic Society), NCGE (National Council for Geographic Education), and NGS (National Geographic Society).) At the same time, U.S. taxpayers have supported vast projects that have mapped the moon, Mars, space, and our entire planet to great specificity. Roads, communication networks, buildings and grounds, water resources, and their unseen underground infrastructure and subsurface geology were all being electronically mapped. Briefly flashed on a television audience's screen were the reconnaissance images of Cuban missile silos. Strategic, defense, and space mapping were silently developing new modes of mapping and cartography. But we tend to interpret these issues to ourselves as "political" even when they have obvious *geographic* dimensions. Geography may be everywhere, but it's still underemphasized in U.S. social studies. Even James Percoco, beloved history teacher in *A Passion for the Past*, in describing a model unit in his applied history class, selects utterly geographic themes as his framework for the unit, reproduced below.

Immigration, Migration, and City Life in America

- Millions move from farm to city between the Civil War and World War I; over 25 million immigrants arrive; southern blacks begin migration to northern and midwestern cities.
- Growth of urban ethnic neighborhoods, institutions, trades, occupations: e.g., Chinatown and Little Italy.
- Resurgence of nativism against hyphenated Americans; controls and restrictions on immigration; Chinese Exclusion Act, 1882.
- Urban population soars: the great cities, e.g., New York, Chicago, and hundreds of smaller cities (e.g., Bridgeport, Toledo); by 1920 census, the majority of Americans live in urban centers.

- Attractions of city life: lights, water, sewers, schools, libraries, museums, dance halls, concert halls, theatres.
- The underside: noise, crime, pollution, poverty, squalor (Jacob Riis photos); racial and ethnic conflicts; start of flight to "streetcar suburbs."
- The need for services and defenders; the rise and workings of ethnic political bosses and mechanics; Tammany Hall.

(Percoco 1998, 44)

Percoco's choice of illustrating this particular history unit bolsters my slogan: "Geography is everywhere!" If it is indeed everywhere, how do we develop geographic questions? What types of ideas constitute geographic inquiry?

Well, there are the basics . . . where will I live, work, visit? What are the nearby resources, family networks, water, hospitals, schools? These very basic questions drive most human movements and are central to Percoco's unit.

Before subsistence farming and settlement took hold, geographic questions were even more highly related to survival: where is there water? Where will we be safe? Where is there game? Where are the edible plants located and in what seasons? Perhaps with the sense of "control" over nature, a lessening of the tension over spatial matters took hold. Since rooting culture in agriculture, we have turned to different types of questions, dismissing those of our more uncertain nomadic past as insignificant. Or perhaps because the questions are so basic, we forget to consider them important. Yet each day, the small triumphs of spatial behavior are essential to the new survival activities. The commuting rituals, parking, arriving on time, delivering on time, and carving out spaces for one's work, home, and recreation are constant preoccupations. While these types of questions are central to our lives, spatial behavior, and decision making, they are less often considered in social studies, even though they are the questions that have driven and shaped prehistory and history.

But there are broader questions than just the basics. Now we must wonder, how long can we stay here before we can't stay any longer? In other words, how do we guard against fouling the global nest? What are the spatial aspects of environmental and social problems we face by living where and how we do? How will that affect taxes? What are the resources worth saving? How do we balance a consumer society and the need for jobs against environmental impacts that will impair our survival? How can we manage growth? Is there a limit on how much land and resource base humans can use without tipping the balance and losing the very ecosystems that sustain us?

Inherent in all of these questions are the more visible aspects of spatial behavior and manifestation upon the land, sea, and atmosphere: the built environment. Is it more efficient to concentrate in cities and let the country-side serve its needs? Where do we locate the next middle school, the new day-care center, the hardware chain, the gas station, the assisted living community? In fact, how should our communities look? How can we make them socially and environmentally sustainable?

One of my favorite ironies about water issues came from the letters to the editor of a local Cape Cod paper during the 1980s. "I don't know what all the fuss is about," an octogenarian complained, "We have enough water in this town to last twenty years!" To him, there was no problem; for my fifteen-year-old sophomores, it wasn't quite far-thinking enough!

A significant case in point is the Quabbin Reservoir in western Massachusetts. Early in the twentieth century, the need for water to the metropolitan Boston area caused purveyors to look uphill. That essentially meant looking west, since Boston sits at the mouth of the Charles River and Boston Harbor. Water moves downhill. Finding small towns nestled near the Connecticut River, one of New England's longest and largest, a plan to relocate the hill people and divert the Swift River was developed. In *Letting Swift River Go*, by Jane Yolen, a children's story about the plan, the Quabbin Reservoir's story is told. From the reservoir, the water is pumped and piped 150 miles to the greater Boston area. This isn't unusual, it's become typical, but so many questions remain as a result.

What happened to the residents of the towns now submerged by the Quabbin? That question intrigued historical documentary filmmaker Ken Burns, who produced the Quabbin Visitors' Center video. What most Bostonians didn't know until recently is that 150 miles west of their city, a 120-square-mile watershed area of zero population density protects the water and health of those in the 40-square-mile metropolitan service area. Where does the water go once it's been used? Those who recall the Dukakis/Bush election of 1988 may remember the environmental and political stink about Boston Harbor.

What happens as Boston grows and needs even more water? Well, plans to divert water directly from the Connecticut River raised the ire of citizens who conducted a study group and recommended that the water purveyor check its own infrastructure for leaks. Since the system had been designed and built so long ago—of pipes made from wood—it stood to reason that replacing the lines would increase yield while being more cost effective and environmentally sound!

That's a spatial problem and not an uncommon one. The issue has sparked nationally recognized curricula for each grade level, published by the Massachusetts Water Resource Authority (see references section). In other regions, flooding and regional planning are even more critical. Water issues in the western U.S., the Middle East, North Africa, and China are even more complex, politically charged, and historically significant.

Globally, housing shortages and traffic congestion are major issues. We see the increase of gated communities while traditional urban neighborhoods are allowed to slide into decay. Here's the current-day picture of Percoco's great cities in decline a hundred years later. Archeology and history tells us that cities continue to flourish, layer upon layer, so urban planners will apparently continue to have GIS work. Given the relative lack of interest or inquisitiveness into matters geographic in the U.S., there remains a burgeoning need for spatial analysis and planning as higher populations put more pressure on existing natural resources, agriculture, and infrastructure of all kinds. GIS skills are highly sought after in the workplace, and GIS-skilled technicians are in extremely high demand (see the GIS Jobs Clearing-house at <www.gjc.org>).

Is GIS Just Another Technology Fad?

It's important to ask this critical question of every technology. There are some technologies that are nice, but they don't really need to be part of the curriculum. GIS is the tool of choice for those who are trying to answer some of the questions I've described. As the questions become more pressing due to population pressures, the need for those trained in asking geographic questions and using database and digital information to answer them grows as well. The estimated growth rate of GIS-related jobs is staggering, yet schools are in the dark about what GIS is, let alone how it might fit into a curriculum, especially a social studies curriculum based on a past when such analytical tools were nonexistent.

GIS is an analytical tool for comparing vast amounts of information in relational databases using geolocations as the common field references. A georeference—some reference to a place on the planet—can locate the information whether on the ground, in the ground, in the atmosphere, or in space. The georeference can be

> • a **point** (such as a coordinate of latitude/longitude or a street address)
>
> —— a **line** (such as a road, a pipeline, or a boundary)
>
> □ or a **polygon** (such as a plot of land, a statistical unit like a census block, or a raster square in a digital image).

A map is a representation of various features using these basic components (see Figure 1–2). Towns have had their tax maps (cadastral maps) digitized. The U.S. Geological Survey has had their contour and topographic information digitized. The Census Bureau's information has been digitized for quite some time, and has been "packaged" by software ventures in map formats for the past two censuses (see <www.census.gov>). Real estate and marketing industries have adapted GIS to their specific needs; local and county governments, states, and the U.S. all have mapping systems that coordinate these massive and burgeoning data-based information systems. Said to characterize the Information Age and its economy, treatments of these turn-of-the-millennium phenomena are relatively absent in social studies classrooms, primarily because textbooks and the accompanying tests don't cover more current and immediate issues.

The Future of Social Studies and GIS' Role

With this book, we're trying to bridge more than one gap. One of the traditional gaps in social studies is the discipline-bound gap between geography and history. While much energy behind the movement to integrate GIS into schools is focused on geography, we actually see GIS as an interdisciplinary application. Many U.S. teachers currently using GIS in classrooms are science teachers conducting environmental studies. GIS is particularly well-suited to representing environmental information. In Canada, most of the uptake is in geography and social studies classrooms. There are growing numbers of historic and archeological studies utilizing GIS to track antiquity resources, historic movements, and other cultural features as the National Park Service (NPS) and NSF-funded historic and archeological research is applied to on-the-ground restoration and preservation projects.

Rather than engage in a discipline war, let's focus on what is developmentally appropriate for students. In his *Mapmaking with Children: Sense of Place Education for the Elementary Years* (1998), David Sobel traces the spatial and social development of children by investigating their play in "special places" and how to expand upon their natural interests in school. As children move into middle school age, they ride bicycles or buses, beginning to expand their environments independently. Today's "digital" generation uses these same natural instincts in the unnatural settings of computer games that are designed like mazes where players must decide and select a route in order to avoid being eaten, blasted, or otherwise annihilated by a hidden force of evil in the game. Like Sobel, I believe that students need real, or what I call *actual*, experience in the world in order to fully develop intellectually. Sobel (1996, 1997) has also written emphatically about developmental issues supporting children's play in natural settings and opposing their obsession with computer games. I quite agree, and have consistently written that children need *actual* experiences in order to apply *virtual* technologies with a critical perspective and ethical practice.

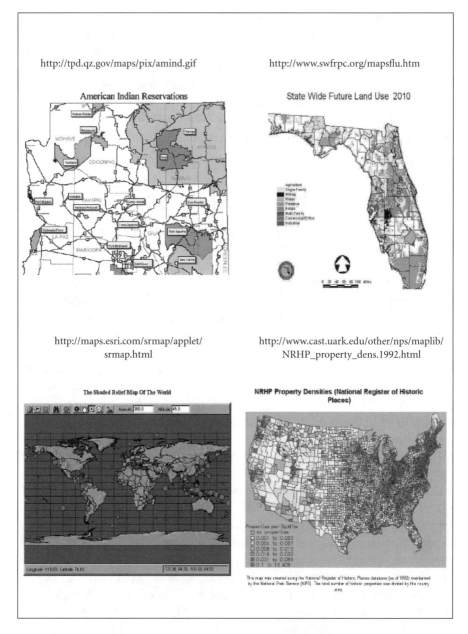

Figure 1–2. *GIS Maps.* Note that in the world GNP (1989) map, countries are polygons, capital cities are points, and major rivers are lines.

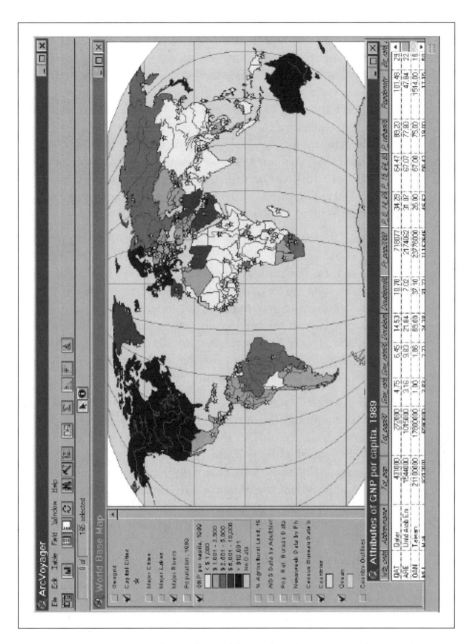

Figure 1–2. *GIS Maps.* Note that in the world GNP (1989) map, countries are polygons, capital cities are points, and major rivers are lines.

Once children move into the middle school years, they are consumed by a desire to explore and to find their own place in the world. Children of this age are constantly exploring social as well as physical space. Given, though, that many adolescents are also learning to operate in cyberspace, an opportunity to express their mastery of these new spaces is utterly age-appropriate. Not only that, but to the degree that adolescents may use these skills to contribute to their communities and take a responsible part in co-constructing those communities, we should find ways to involve them in prosocial activities. Using GIS can open pathways to integrate adolescents' natural proclivities into positive and valued contributions.

All of the projects described in this book are examples of this kind of opportunity. In *A Passion for the Past* (1998), Percoco reminds us,

> When studying history you need to be able to grasp something tangible and the textbooks don't allow that to happen—most of them have left the story out of history. The study of history requires a spiritual connection with the past, an ability to let your mind go back in time to see, feel, and in some cases taste the eras that were before our time. The way I teach is centered on this extension of the curriculum: getting students to look beyond the textbook and beyond the classroom—out into the world. As I put closure on the first day of class, I point out the window and say, "It's not in here where you're going to do your learning, it's out there." (7)

Percoco refers to his teaching as "applied history" in which he infuses the skills and practices of public history to engage students in participatory history projects and service. With GIS that service can extend more deeply into the community's social and environmental health, which are integrally related. If we want socially and environmentally healthy communities, we must learn how to help students develop not only a sense of place, but also a sense of responsibility to the community. This moves beyond "a sense of place" to "a place in the community." It is through our interactions with people and places that we constitute community.

Paul Theobald, in his book *Teaching the Commons* (1997), describes the importance of community-based education:

> Schools ought to attend more consciously to their physical place on earth and the social, political and economic demands that surround it. Doing so would render the entire school experience more meaningful and, in the process, would contribute in a small, though not insignificant, way to a cultural healing desperately needed in American society. (1)

In *Community and the Politics of Place* (1990), Daniel Kemmis describes "barn-raising" as a time when the entire community, regardless of how each may have felt about another's politics or personal frailties, was needed. The common hearth of the community has long since vanished. There are only vestiges of this left in postindustrial society. Let's be honest about this and recognize it; today's students are not living in the same world as those born at mid-century. There is ever more reason to forge more meaning, connection, and durability between the multigenerational and multicultural populations of our communities, specifically the social and environmental health and sustainability of our common future.

Expanding the Social Studies Landscape

One of the ways the National Council for the Social Studies (NCSS) has met the "discipline war" issue has been to derive the multidisciplinary themes of social studies. The ten themes that form the framework of NCSS' social studies standards are more fully described at <www.ncss.org/standards/exec.html>:

I. Culture	VI. Power, Authority and Governance
II. Time, Continuity and Change	VII. Production, Distribution and Consumption
III. People, Places and Environments	VIII. Science, Technology and Society
IV. Individual Development and Identity	IX. Global Connections
V. Individuals, Groups and Institutions	X. Civic Ideals and Practices

These themes represent the broad brush of social studies; not just of history and geography, but also of economics (which, after all, does motivate human behavior and affairs), political science, anthropology, sociology, and psychology. Social studies is a *multi*discipline. You won't find this word in a dictionary—yet—but as the twentieth century drew to a close, the impacts of environmental science and integrative technologies like GIS had even changed the traditional "disciplinary" landscape. Geography reemerged onto the social studies scene in the 1980s, fueled by the National Geographic Society and its partners in GENIP. I was one of some four hundred teachers nationwide who participated in the NGS Summer Institutes at the NGS headquarters in Washington, D.C., where we spent six weeks studying and generating geographic educational infusion plans and activities. Still, in the twenty-first century, geography must battle its way into social studies curricula and departments across the U.S. while neighboring Canada, in the British tradition, places geography at the center of each grade level in the curriculum. As I mentioned earlier, the movement to standardize and centrally locate geography in the U.S. curriculum is still in process; GIS software developer ESRI has joined the GENIP effort in that movement.

Because it is central to understanding my purpose in writing this book about GIS integration, I'll confess a certain affection for geography, but as a social studies teacher, I believe it more important to *listen to students*, and select from the multidiscipline of social studies to meet their needs. This is how we began to teach geography in the 1970s when no one was teaching geography—our students needed it, period.

The regional technical high school where I taught drew students from fifteen towns and, therefore, several different junior high or middle schools. After a year of teaching this particular population, I noticed that the one critical gap in their social studies preparation was any sense of geography. Therefore, it was *their need* that moved me to teach geography. With a dim recollection of teaching in the time "BS"—Before Standards—I believe that teachers felt more freedom to respond to students' needs. (In an M.Ed. curriculum course at a state college, a novice teacher asked, "What did teachers do before the standards?" We all burst out laughing, quipping, "Oh, nothing, we just waited around until they came to tell us what to do!")

If we are listening to students and filling their needs from our broad multidiscipline, we are leading as sure as any other policy-driven, industry-based, top-down movement leads. And our job is leading students and developing them, not enriching the testing or textbook industries. One solution is to get out of the classroom and into the field, and GIS is one technology useful in that movement.

Lacking Logic, Seeking Synthesis

One of the haunting questions since the 9/11/01 attacks was the repeated question, "Why do they hate us?" The fact that Americans as a whole and social studies students in particular had no idea why Americans were targeted by terrorism indicates not just a lack of awareness, but a lack of synthesis of information. Competing logics among the many social studies disciplines leads to a condition of "asynthesis." In *Pedagogy of the Oppressed* (1968), Paulo Freire wrote about the problem of "ahistoricity," a condition a social studies teacher educator found among her students at Boston College that manifested itself in beliefs that "that's just the way it is." The professor had posed the question, "Why is it that our class isn't diverse at all in its population?" When students could only respond, "That's just the way it is," she became determined to awaken critical inquiry and thinking among her students, never to allow them to fall back to their complacent *ahistorical* beliefs. Her goal became one of never allowing unexamined social conditions, but developing habits of mind that would always question "how it *became* the way it is."

Since 9/11/01, Wendell Berry has articulated this lulled complacency, this magical belief in the inherent "goodness" of technology, of ever-enhanced consumer goods. If one part of the human population decides it is "chosen" or has a birthright to unlimited health and wealth, its education is quite obviously incomplete. It is incomplete by design, by cooption, and by a desire to cast a blind eye toward the rest of humanity and the planet.

There is a lack of synthesis of logics; of the logic of *economics*—from the Greek, the management (*nomos*) of the home (*oikos*)—and the logic of *ecology*—from the Greek, the science of the home as habitat.

By placing an inordinate weight upon the *chrono*logy of a narrow stream of history, social studies has allowed itself—a multidiscipline—to be defined by the testing and textbook industries who then "measure" the efficiency of student consumption of its goods even while those students live in a dream world of television commercials, media hype, and virtual reality games. Like chronology, *techno*logy has also become an opiate. We are ever receiving messages about what we should own or wear, messages about what to value, what to think, but alas, not *how* to think, not how to outsmart the capitalists who drive the desire-manufacturing.

One wonders how, in fact, the messages of a living earth—the *geo*logic, the *bio*logic, the *hydro*logic, are even heard through the cacophony. Does the student know the land, know the water, know the plant life that supports him or her? Did the history lessons cover the conservation and environmental movements? The nuclear freeze movement? By neglecting other than the *chrono*logic, we have, as Sandra Postel has put it, very precisely missed the point.

"Mapping" GIS onto NCSS' Ten Themes

Taking a closer look at the NCSS' ten themes, GIS has a role in more than half of them directly, and arguably *all* of them indirectly, since human experience is grounded on the planet and every political unit requires some kind of spatial frame, even if it's a "neural" or communications network.

I. Culture*

II. Time, Continuity and Change*

III. People, Places and Environments*

IV. Individual Development and Identity

V. Individuals, Groups and Institutions

VI. Power, Authority and Governance

VII. Production, Distribution and Consumption*

VIII. Science, Technology and Society*

IX. Global Connections*

X. Civic Ideals and Practices

The six themes above that are starred represent those that are most directly linked to geographic or spatial applications, and therefore could be enhanced by integrating GIS information. Again, however, I emphasize that GIS must be presented within a critical and ethical framework and that it be used to support civic ideals and practices. In the case study chapters, we will demonstrate the thematic connections with GIS applications.

Why Does NCSS Have a "Science, Technology, and Society" Theme?

If we consider the students as the starting point, let us consider the historical context of the students' lives. Students entering freshman year in high school in the year 2000 were born in 1986. If their first political awareness awakened at perhaps ten years of age, they may have recollections of the Persian Gulf war, the highly televised "technological" war. Shortly thereafter, for almost a year, the Monica Lewinsky affair, school violence, and the Columbine High School shootings dominated media and, therefore, national attention.

This is always a sobering exercise for a social studies educator. By the time one has trained to teach, one's life and experience are substantially longer than those of students; one's frame of reference is much broader, and one has found strategies for interpreting new information—filtering out the bad, keeping the good.

But again, let us try to interpret the world from the students' perspective. Surely, the major effect of the media on students at the turn of the century is the omnipresence of technologically mediated information. From my work with technical high school students, a focus on technology and its role and effects on society were essential to my students' connection with history. It gave students an entry point into history, since they are children of a technological age but without an understanding of how those technologies had evolved. How had all of this material culture evolved?

Few science teachers have time to teach the history of science and technology. Without that understanding, there is a disconnect between the reality of students' lives and their immediate surroundings, whose history seems utterly remote. The so-called Dark Ages were actually times of much incremental technological advance. Those developing technological advances were not among the elite, so their mechanical and technological developments were not glorified (see particularly Dava Sobel's *Longitude* [1996]). How difficult for us to imagine a historic perspective in which a Bill Gates would have been considered a tinkerer. But it is critically important to understand that the significance of technology has become glorified in this century since the industrial revolution.

Few history teachers address the history of science and technology, but the NCSS recognizes the significance of a critical examination of the relationships of science, technology, and society (STS). I looked at the NCSS' ten themes only after deciding what to teach, but found myself intrigued by the questions inherent in STS. It is certainly from this perspective that I believe GIS should be examined and understood before it is used or practiced. Where else will students develop a critical perspective on technology? There is a great fear among those in the STS field that students are simply shaped by the technology and have developed no means by which to evaluate, criticize, or live their lives without it.

Indeed, there is reason for this. Students at a 1998 STS conference shared their beliefs that those without access to the Internet would be unable to participate in a democratic society. We posed the antiapartheid and civil rights movements as counterpoints. The former had occurred in these students' elementary years.

While mainstream perspectives label societies as "developed, developing, or underdeveloped," we could just as easily call them "technology dependent" and "technology independent" societies. Certainly those who depend heavily on technological hardware and software do not wish to see themselves as dependent, but it is simply a matter of perspective. Friends in the GIS software business aren't particularly fond of this characterization, or that the technology is not necessarily the key to all problem solving. But I believe we must be able to critique the very tools we use, otherwise we are blinded to their limitations or to the world that remains invisible without the technology. If nothing else, the lessons of 9/11/01 remind us that technology can be the Achilles' heel of the present and future.

"Hands-on"? Balancing the *Actual* and the *Virtual*

Given this rather prickly perspective, I also maintain that computer-aided instruction—even GIS, with its amazing analytical potential—does not constitute "hands-on" learning or engage what Howard Gardner describes as "bodily-kinesthetic" intelligence in *Frames of Mind* (1983). Until there are definitive MRI studies of computer use and brain functioning, I will maintain that there is a distinction between use of computer applications and *actual* hands-on experience. While I have to concede that there is a unique skill set involved in mastering computer software applications, and that these can be very complex, I would compare them to the skills of writing rather than to a more physical interaction or Gardner's "bodily-kinesthetic" experience.

When we sit at the computer, we are more engaged mentally than physically. In fact, we should all fear for the amount of time our bodies are *not* engaged in activity because we are sitting at computers, becoming less fit and subjected to direct cathode rays. That said, computer games designed for children involve their natural instincts to seek and find. These games are what I call *virtual* simulations of the *actual* experience children routinely practice in their play.

For GIS to be useful or meaningful, I feel it is best grounded in *actual* experience. In fact, "ground truthing," or comparing a map to features actually on the ground, was one of the components of a school project described in the case studies. In Chapter 8, Getting Behind the Map, students ground truthed satellite images. The service students provided was to ground truth a product of a billion-dollar mapping technology, meaning that they did field-work to verify satellite imagery. This was only one aspect of their yearlong "capstone" project. In most of the schools I visited, students had *actual* experience in the community that was then connected to the *virtual* map.

Let's put this discussion in its historical context. First is the end of millennium concept of "diversity," a value whose source derives from E. O. Wilson's description of ecological relationships as dynamic and interconnected systems of biodiversity (Wilson 1992). Since his introduction of the term, "diversity" has been applied to both social and economic usage. Geography and history have been and are in the process of integrating the concept across the social studies. There has been a call from institutional leaders in economics, ecology, and education to design institutional models based on living systems rather than mechanical systems.

Second, while there is a generational phenomenon of students "growing up digital," it is not a whole generational phenomenon; it is a class-bound generational phenomenon (Tapscott 1998). And while many in this new generation may view technology as humanity's salvation, they are still youth that require wholistic actual experiences in order to develop fully and to use their skills wisely. Wisdom is not inherent within computer skills. In fact, we may more easily identify wisdom from skill by balancing the actual with the virtual in education, as well as balancing the spatial with the temporal. Facility with technology must be balanced with a development of responsibility through critical thinking and ethical decision making. There have been too many technology-savvy adolescent killers for us to assume that students with computer skills are adequately integrated with their communities.

Third, if we miss the historic imperative this turn of the century presents, we will surely have lost the mission of social studies to develop citizens capable of assuming the rights and responsibilities of democratic participation. Throughout the book, I will call for and illustrate evidence of and opportunities to develop students through conducting social studies, the hands-on, applied history, geography, sociology, anthropology, political science, economics that can be researched and represented by students using GIS.

The GIS Connection: Where Is GIS?

On the companion CD, we have an activity called "Where Is GIS?" that may be used as an introduction for students to discover GIS using the Internet. Try it!

2

Is There Any Spatially Intelligent
Life on This Planet?

As we transition into a new century, we have an unique opportunity to reflect upon the historic context of the twentieth century's shifting paradigms and perspectives on history, geopolitics, and what has come to be known as cultural and biological diversity. From this new vantage point, how will we view the function of education in communities and the directions in which we might proceed? It is as if we have reached a type of divide, a horizon or vantage point from which the experiences of the past hundred orbits might redirect the next.

Asking the Question, "Is This My Problem as a Social Studies Teacher?"

If anything is to have been learned from the shifts that characterized the twentieth century and the horrifying events of September 11, 2001, the major problem for educators should be how to realign our goals and curriculum to refocus our youth toward sustainable human communities worldwide. By 2001, we humans had exceeded six billion in population. With our unprecedented numbers, connecting our youth appears to be our only *viable* option since, as we have seen, other options threaten our viability. Claims of a "global economy" ring hollow across many nations, where subsistence agriculture continues to support a majority of the human race. What we should learn from the attack on the World Trade Center is that the world includes the biosphere and all of the members of the human race, not just the few who have invested for themselves. The human race is only as strong as our weakest link, so complacency and arrogance are no excuse for ignoring the conditions of our entire species.

It was during the past century that humans began to understand our limits, both technologically and ecologically. By the end of the twentieth century and its millennium, multiple social events and movements had altered the spatial frameworks of human behavior from its previous configurations. In one century, two "world wars" were waged, independence movements had transformed former colonies, and large sociopolitical entities had formed and collapsed again into smaller states; "nations" were born.

Some identify the dawn of the "Modern Age" with the successful *Sputnik I* launching in October of 1957. For this discussion, I will refer to the period 1950–1980 as the "Space Age," and the period between 1980 and 2010 as the "Information Age" to delineate technological periods in the way the terms "Stone Age" and "Bronze Age" have been used. I do, however, use these terms almost tongue-in-cheek, as my personal view is that the cultures proclaiming these "ages" are so technology dependent as to have to categorize human experience by technological development; we could just as easily choose historical periods of art, music, or spirituality as the measures, with the understanding that *any* classification is culture-bound in its references.

Implicit in our naming of "Space" (uppercase "S") has been the assumption that we are discussing "outer space" or extraterrestrial space. Another implicit assumption underlying our explorations into Space was the belief that we could colonize it somehow. Entire genres of science fiction novels and films give testimony to those beliefs. But our *actual* journeys into Space and our *actual* deployment of nuclear weapons have brought us humans up short in terms of their utility to the species. Both of these former technological "frontiers" have yielded rather definitive dead ends. Yet it has been those scientists at the forefront of these technologies that have returned from those frontiers with renewed respect for the biological, the ecological, the human aspects of what and where we are—spatially, temporally, environmentally, and developmentally. Upon his death in 1896, Alfred Nobel, inventor of dynamite, bequeathed annual prizes for peace, sciences, economics, and literature. Albert Einstein, 1921 winner of the Nobel prize in physics, whose theories led to the development of the atomic bomb, later implored political leaders and citizens to be vigilant about the uses of scientific and technological discoveries. Kevin Kelley, in his book *The Home Planet* (1988), presents the views (both photographic and linguistic) of many members of the international Association of Space Explorers, astronauts who have each experienced space flight in Earth's orbit (see Figure 2–1).

From space I saw Earth—indescribably beautiful with the scars of national boundaries gone. (Muhammad Ahmad Faris, Syria)

Figure 2–1. *NASA Image* <http://earthobservatory.nasa.gov/Newsroom/BlueMarble>

The first day or so, we all pointed to our countries. The third or fourth day we were pointing to our continents. By the fifth day we were aware of only one Earth. (Sultan Bin Salman al-Saud, the Kingdom of Saudi Arabia)

My mental boundaries expanded when I viewed the earth against a black and uninviting vacuum, yet my country's rich traditions had conditioned me to look beyond the man-made boundaries and prejudices. One does not have to undertake a space flight to come by this feeling. (Rakesh Sharma, India)

After an orange cloud—formed as a result of a dust storm over the Sahara and caught up by air currents—reached the Philippines and settled there with rain, I understood that we are all sailing in the same boat. (Vladimir Kovalyonok, USSR)

During a space flight, the psyche of each astronaut is reshaped. Having seen the sun, the stars, and our planet, you become more full of life, softer. You begin to look at all living things with greater trepidation and you begin to be more kind and patient with the people around you. At least that is what happened to me. (Boris Volynov, USSR)

In short, there is no more viable frontier suitable for colonization. Now what is left is to live within the limits of planet earth.

Shifting the Focus

In comments she delivered to teachers at the National Geographic Summer Institute of 1989, geographer and national curriculum consultant Barbara Winston characterized the shifts in turn-of-the-century understandings and curricula as these:

Euro-centered	→ to →	GLOBAL-centered
Group-centered	→ to →	SPECIES-centered
Nation-state-centered	→ to →	PLANET-centered
Anthropo-centered	→ to →	ECOSYSTEM-centered
Past-centered	→ to →	PAST/PRESENT/FUTURE-centered
Information-centered	→ to →	ISSUE- or PROBLEM-centered
Spectator-centered	→ to →	PARTICIPANT-centered

In addition, Winston described some of the new awarenesses of conceptual change that would facilitate the shifts she identified. Those she described as:

PERSPECTIVE consciousness

STATE OF THE PLANET consciousness

CROSS- and MULTICULTURAL awareness

GLOBAL SYSTEM awareness

Awareness of CHOICES and opportunities for ACTION

As I reflect on these from the vantage point of a new century, I see many of Winston's descriptions as prescient. I see GIS as useful to the practice of conducting social studies in moving toward this goal. I also see from reflecting on Winston's words that they have been a helpful way of understanding the shifts as a continuum along which we may be progressing at different rates, but that, in so many ways, much of the movement is influenced by the images and maps we have at hand through various media, but especially the new imaging techniques.

Also unique to the twentieth century, increased communication has enabled us to learn of greater diversity and similarity through using more connective media than had ever before been possible. Thus, the concept of diversity has merged as both biologically and culturally emblematic from both ecological and multicultural studies.

We can now aerially photograph, map, and measure every inch of the planet; indeed, the planet itself became "finite" once we were able to see it in its place from space; and so, we have seen our own place as well. What is left now is understanding how to live within it—within those limits that we had never actually seen, when its limits were more abstract: a globe on a stand or a sphere in a diagram. Now indisputable photographs show a planet suspended in vastly open space. Satellite images and aerial photographs are registered hourly for a variety of purposes and are available for integration with GIS maps for weather, communication, and surveillance.

Our understanding of our place in space has led to a deeper value on our earthly places and in understanding those places both within a planet-bound system of systems, and as nested systems within systems (as in solar systems within galaxies within groups of galaxies, and so on). From this turn-of-the-century perspective, a return to earth has been the unexpected result of the technological developments that took us as far as off of the planet, and out to others.

Space cowboyism and intergalactic colonization now relegated to science fiction, we must examine our nomadic past and its associated knowledge and skills and reassess them in light of our more recent sedentary past, present, and future *within* our given ecological limits. Our previous strategies for inhabitation have been nomadism, slash-and-burn, and sedentary agriculture. In some regions, these have been (and are) combined over wide areas. Where nomadism has been abandoned, cities have grown, some into "civilizations."

Knowing Our Place

In previous research with college students (Alibrandi 1993), I analyzed written papers and hand-drawn images to unearth the roots of internal representations of place; to understand the nature of personal and cultural constructions of place and the individual's place within it, not as apart from it. Having taught high school for so many years, I shouldn't have been surprised by my findings, but I was. The most frequently mentioned connection to places was direct physical interaction with them. Climbing, swimming, digging and all manner of hands-on learning and engagement with places was overwhelmingly present in people's descriptions of their favorite places. In addition, the temporal experience in those places over time was a recurrent theme. People attributed qualities to places, and for the (mostly North) American students, the values of peace, security, and freedom were the most often connected to favorite places. As well, students attributed places with their own numinosity or *genius loci*—in other words, the place had its own spirit. It is a matter of attention, of metacognition, of listening to our instinctual knowledge that is required for us to connect deeply with places. This is, however, a difficult task here in the Information Age. Human attention is constantly diverted away from "knowing one's own mind" toward the messages of external media.

The knowing of places is grounded in lived experience, in day-to-day spatial operations. I use the term *grounded* as Lakoff and Johnson in *Metaphors We Live By* (1980) used it to describe the locations of lived experience, "As in the case of orientational metaphors, basic ontological metaphors are grounded by virtue of *systematic correlates within our experience*" (58) [emphasis theirs]. By ontological, they mean the development or evolution of the self.

For this discussion, let's simply establish that people's lived experiences in the physical world are important to their understanding *of* the world, not just in terms of spatial behavior, but in terms of all types of metaphors and mental constructs. The patterns seen in the natural or lived world are the basis of the *pattern recognition* essential to all learning. Gardner describes this as the symbology that can transfer learning by one type of intelligence (say, spatial) to another (say, linguistic). I will explore and expand this in greater depth in the section on spatial cognition. But by going a step further than constructing a sense of "self," I am proposing with the practice of conducting social studies that in schools we would simultaneously coconstruct community and self, thereby building in an understanding of community-as-self in which one's identity and survival are synonymous with one's community.

While curriculum specialists debate about the ways to develop "citizens," the communities *in which* those citizens live, vote, pollute or don't pollute, recreate, reproduce, produce, and consume are seen somehow as being constructed by "others." This *disconnect between student citizenship and life within a community* is the missing link in social studies education. If we cannot develop in students a connection to communities, then there is no sense of place, of history, or of wanting to preserve or conserve a community's social or environmental health. This sense of "knowing one's place"—in the universe, in the solar system, on the planet, in an ecosystem, in a community—is central to learning who one is.

The school projects described in the following chapters capture how a new sense of place and students' essential roles in their communities can be facilitated through incorporating GIS. While GIS may not be necessary to accomplish identity with community, it served to create mutual relationships of capacity across school and community through its power to literally "put oneself on the map."

"Finding Home"

Out of the overwhelming communications media, come the small messages, remembered by those who still listen to them, and by those who traveled off of the planet, to the furthest extent of human spatial limits. The essential message is one that comes from both the ancient depths and the outer limits of human experience, and is about "finding home." Those who have traveled into orbit remark,

> Instead of an intellectual search, there was suddenly a very deep gut feeling that something was different. It occurred when looking at Earth and seeing this blue-and-white planet floating there, and knowing it was orbiting the Sun, seeing that Sun, seeing it set in the background of the very deep black and velvety cosmos, seeing—rather, knowing for sure—that there was a purposefulness of flow, of energy, of time, of space in the cosmos—that it was beyond man's rational ability to understand, that suddenly there was a nonrational way of understanding that had been beyond my previous experience.
>
> There seems to be more to the universe than random, chaotic, purposeless movement of a collection of molecular particles.
>
> On the return trip home, gazing through 240,000 miles of space toward the stars and the planet from which I had come, I suddenly experienced the universe as intelligent, loving, harmonious.
>
> We went to the moon as technicians; we returned as humanitarians.
> (Edgar Mitchell in Kelley 1988, 138)

Practicing Democracy—In Communities? States? Regions?

> Living in a place—the notion has been around for decades and has usually been dismissed as provincial, backward, dull, and possibly reactionary. But new dynamics are at work. The mobility that has characterized American life is coming to a close. As Americans begin to stay put, it may give us the first opening in over a century to give participatory democracy another try. (Snyder 1995, 231)

This practice of democracy is one that is situated within regions and places. It is in fact the struggles to live together within ever more crowded population densities that become interpreted as issues or crises. Here, Snyder leads us toward a renewed understanding of a participatory democracy, one built upon bioregional polities. In the last quarter of the twentieth century, the U.S. Department of the Interior began moving toward the "Watershed Approach" in response to the EPA's problems in dealing with nonpoint source pollution, or pollution that can't be geographically pinpointed. The spatial problem that arose from trying to isolate unbounded pollution sources led to watershed-based solutions. This turn-of-the-century understanding of spatial, ecological, or bioregional organization runs into political constructs of space.

GIS professor Akhlaque Haque, in a recent article, "GIS, Public Service and the Issue of Democratic Governance," states, "If information is power . . . and if community is built through dialogue, then GIS permits both to emerge for those who would otherwise have no voice and no space for action" (Haque 2001, 261). Haque acknowledges that the wealthy have access to GIS and use it; corporations and developers may have interests that conflict with those of citizens and the EPA, so he calls for a widespread use of GIS specifically aimed at participatory democracy.

Other Frames of Political Geography

With the development of the United Nations as a global forum, the political entities represented there became more focused on preserving the viability of their own units and of those they recognized. Thus, the protection of the member nation-states as viable political entities became a primary interest. Geographer Bernard Nietschmann (1988) theorized, though, that in the twentieth century, the reemergence of "nationalism" is based in more ancient cultural concepts of that identity. He assessed that the current political states recognized as "nations" by the United Nations were actually states (or bodies politic), while the concept of nation (derived from *natio, nascio,* being born) indicates a deeper identity and construct. Therefore, in Nietschmann's analysis, each of the current political "states" is actually a multinational state, save for some very few monocultural states that are also congruent with original nations of what he calls a "people" (for example, the Japanese).

Nietschmann labeled the conflicts born of clashes between the nations and the political states as part of the "Third World War." Geographers recognize the forces of cohesion as *centripetal* and those of internal fraction as *centrifugal* forces. The latter come into play during civil wars and the former are enhanced when attacks appear from external sources. While history would bear that no political entity lasts forever, there is still a persistent desire to retain existing boundaries and protect them, now that they are recognized by the United Nations. Naturally, those political states participating in the UN are interested in perpetuating themselves as viable political entities.

But terrorism, which is what the political states have labeled this "nationalistic" resistance or resurgence, indicates that neither systematized pluralism nor democracy has yet been achieved in areas where intense nationalism is present. While this can be understood geographically as the *centrifugal* force, it is framed politically as state vs. enemy of the state. This is one of the great failings of not teaching geography; the concepts of centripetal and centrifugal forces are not seen as predictable human patterns to be addressed politically. Therefore our social construction of (these geographically predictable) events caused by these centrifugal and centripetal forces are framed as "war" or "terrorism," when there are certainly more *viable* geopolitical solutions available.

If Geography Is Everywhere, Where Is Spatial Cognition?

While volumes have been written on spatial cognition (the "invisible intelligence"), behavior, mental representations of space (known as "mental maps"), environmental perception and geographic knowledge acquisition, virtually none of it has reached the average social studies teacher. (The works of Yi-Fu-Tuan, Roger Downs and David Stea, Reginald Golledge, Lynn Liben, and others are listed in the reference section.) While knowledge acquisition theory and cognitive science have altered the field of cognitive psychology, the research remains obscure from pre- and inservice teachers. One inservice theme that arose in the late 1990s was the "brain and learning" concept, but a lack of understanding of spatial cognition persists.

"Spatial intelligence," as Howard Gardner calls it, gets lost in the love-hate relationship of tradition vs. innovation and hierarchy vs. equity for several reasons in education in the U.S. How can I level this assertion about tradition vs. innovation and hierarchy vs. equity as central to issues of spatial intelligence, cognition, learning, and teaching?

First, the tradition vs. innovation syndrome is a battle between the existing curriculum and what I've called the "forbidden curriculum." The forbidden curriculum is anything that doesn't appear in national or state frameworks, competencies, or guidelines and is therefore unsanctioned or, to some, forbidden. Educators (not "education," that mythical monolith) must, in my view, be responsive to the needs of students. When we learned of environmental issues, should we have ignored them? If South Africa and its apartheid policies weren't in the official curriculum, should we have ignored them? When terrorism reared up in the 1970s, should we social studies teachers have ignored it? One sees that the danger of ignoring the events occurring, their causes, and their effects is that it *actually creates ignorance* when some contend that there is an official curriculum to be addressed. This is at the root of the tradition vs. innovation paradox. Should the educator remain tradition bound? Many of the teacher's external political forces would contend: "Yes!" This problem is further exacerbated by the weight of high-stakes testing, a source of immense anxiety to educators.

On the other hand, the society rewards innovation: innovation in product design, communications, transportation, and so on. Here is the golden carrot: be the first to innovate, design, and market something and you win! Money, status, and probably undeserved reverence are showered upon the innovator. Fact is, many of the innovations require spatial intelligence clearly outside the traditional curriculum. The traditional curriculum has been right-fully criticized as heavily dependent upon linguistic intelligence. Textbooks and the tests that test the textbooks' efficiency of transmission rule the day.

This is where the hierarchy vs. equity issue comes into play: *If* you hap-pen to have spatial abilities and you get through a U.S. education with those abilities still intact *and* you're able to use them to design the next communi-cations goo-gaw, game, unnecessary vehicular adaptation, or, in some cases, useful or lifesaving or life-enhancing device, you can be rich! However, spa-tial ability, randomly distributed across the population and undetected, undervalued, and untaught in any subjects but physical education and industrial arts goes undeveloped, because basically, we don't know how to teach with it, to it, or for it.

The only reason I became at all aware of spatial and bodily-kinesthetic intelligences was because I worked in a technical high school where, for *most* of the students, these were the preferred modes of learning. These students essentially taught me how to teach them by not responding particularly well to a lecture/reading/writing format, but responding very well to mapping, charting, creating time lines, using graphic organizers, building—in short, constructing knowledge actively. Those approaches came to be known over the course of my career as hands-on learning and teaching.

Spatial skills are developed prior to language, and perhaps because of that, we are less able to articulate them—even to recognize, identify, or name them. The infant uses the haptic sense (the sense of touch) to encounter the world before vision is even likely interpreted (90 percent of "vision" being processed in the brain; the eye as organ simply senses light and color). And while the sounds and smells of mother or caregiver become familiar from early in a child's life, it is the haptic and spatial operations and behaviors that are developed first. As children feel comforted, safe, and secure being held, they will also begin to grasp, touch, and navigate within the first three months of life. Comprehensible language is recognized when aural and visual cues can reinforce the target word. Keep in mind, though, that even children blind from birth can navigate in space, develop mental maps and represent (if not picture) spatial arrangements, building layouts, stairwells, city blocks, and abstract spatial concepts—not to mention play instruments, type, compute, and read through the haptic sense.

While much knowledge acquisition theory has been based upon lan-guage acquisition, infants and toddlers actually practice the basic structural components of language as they operate in the physical world through spa-tial behavior and cognition. The most basic components of language, recog-nized as "nodes" and "links," are analogous to—and probably learned first as—spatial behaviors. As infants become able to locate a target ("node"), they will either attempt to grasp it, or, somewhat later, to move toward it. This behavior precedes language production, in which the child seeks the target word (node) from memory. The node-and-link connections in language essentially reflect spatial behavior patterns and location problems that have already been mastered and therefore provide a structure or logic or schematic that can be applied to language. Language acquisition theory is based on repetitions of target words and shared meanings, but the child has already become adept at successfully reaching for, grasping, holding, and moving toward target objects in space.

Because spatial behavior is in many ways "silent" and, in Western cultures, believed to be not as sophisticated as language, it has become forgotten and even ignored as an important skill set. Yet when girls perform less well than boys on specific test skills, we make assumptions about their abilities to learn these skills that are then represented as "male," better, more complex, and (hierarchically) rewarded.

Much has been researched and written about these gender differences. In my teaching experience, I began to try to understand how students—especially girls who excelled at geography—combined their linguistic and spatial intelligences to master geographic content. I conducted longitudinal research with a subset of students from ninth to twelfth grades.

Teacher Research

Again, it was my students who taught me what was needed. I first began teaching in the technical high school when it opened in 1975. At the time, geography was utterly absent from the curriculum save for limited attention in the lower grades. We opened the school with a "progressive" problem-solving approach in social studies. But toward the end of our first year, when my students were collectively deciding on our final unit of study for the year, their lack of basic knowledge of geography stunned me. In a preliminary conversation about our upcoming unit, gross misconceptions about basic political geography came out.

Student: Well, you know, there are different laws in different states like Mexico!

Teacher: Okay, you mean New Mexico? New Mexico is a state.

Student: No, Mexico. They have different laws.

Teacher: Okay, that's true—they have different laws in Mexico, but Mexico is a country, like Canada—in North America there are three countries, Canada, the U.S., and Mexico, right?

(silence)

Teacher: Okay—let me ask a question here. How many states are there in the U.S.?

Students: (guessing) Fifty-two? No, five hundred?

This was June of 1976. I had had these students as ninth graders for a year and was just finding out that not one of them knew that the U.S. had fifty states. That revelation changed my life as a teacher. I continued to question my students during that final month and decided that we needed as a department to address this gap. Our students hailed from fifteen different sending school communities to attend our regional high school. It took two years to convince the department that we needed to institute geography as the ninth-grade curriculum because, I advocated, it would be literally impossible to teach any other social studies if students didn't have a sense of basic geographic concepts and content such as where things were in the world. Finally, in 1978, we began teaching geography to all incoming ninth graders.

Answering the Question: "What are spatial skills, and where would they fit into the curriculum?"

At millions of intersections the world over, in order to conduct everyday life, humans must operate in space. Physical movement, the location of objects, access to objects, resources, people, and places are performed not haphazardly, but with intent, purpose, and some degree of efficiency and grace. The measure of one's ability to function spatially effectively we might call *spatial competence.*

The development of spatial competence (or competencies) requires a system of processes of spatial knowledge acquisition. From experimentation with laboratory rats, Tolman (1948) concluded that in order to operate in space, mobile creatures must retain in memory internal spatial representations that assist them in their spatial operations and decision making in familiar settings. Tolman coined this a "cognitive-type map."

Cognitive maps are internal spatial representations stored in memory in either static or dynamic patterned images of spatial phenomena, experienced or imagined. In other words, they are internally stored as either images or as movie-like sequences. In humans, these cognitive maps may also represent from very familiar to quite foreign abstract places, images, or schematics that may be retrieved for the purpose of planning, travel, searching, wayfinding, or other spatial goals.

Roger Downs and David Stea in their *Maps in Minds* (1977) preferred the term "cognitive mapping" for an internal representation and "cognitive map" for a produced sketch or other product representing spatial phenomena (these would include sketch maps, drawings, or diagrams). Kevin Lynch had pioneered the use of sketch maps in his landmark study, *Image of the*

City (1960). With that study, Lynch fathered the discipline of urban studies and design by asking residents to both sketch and verbally describe their cities. With hundreds of such products drawn from several cities, Lynch derived certain elements as "nodes," "paths," "edges," and "districts" as mental constructs used by residents in their daily operations about the city. These elements compare readily to linguistic elements of "nodes," "links," and other comparable elements. I will draw on this spatial and linguistic comparison in order to frame an understanding of engaging both types of learning (or cognition) in the classroom.

In the studies I conducted, I asked students to produce "your own map" or "your personal representation" of a place. I later referred to the products as "mental maps" in discussing those products. In my own use of sketch maps for educational purposes, I have found additional aspects worthy of a reconsideration of maps as artifacts for portfolio and diagnostic assessment. When, for example, sketch maps are used as artifacts to assess student learning, they serve as indicators of progress in spatial (or geographic) knowledge acquisition. Periodically produced maps demonstrate basic progressions of general-to-specific learning applications. As artifacts, they might be (and have been) analyzed for clues to processes and cultural influences involved in developing spatial competencies.

In their research with first, third, and fifth graders, Vosniadou and Brewer (1992) elicited drawings and descriptions of the earth. Comparing the verbal and graphic representations, they derived composite models they call "Mental Models" at the three developmental stages, demonstrating a progression of conceptual modeling over the elementary grades.

Sketch maps, I propose, then, are always rough drafts, since, with additional experience in the environment or with other inputs or inferences, additional information may be included. Software developers have built upon these mental processes to design GIS functions and features to reflect the skills humans inherently bring to spatial representation. An infinite number of images or attributes could be attached in a person's memory with a specific place or location; images from this perspective or that, light conditions, seasonal views, current ownership or values, historic uses or values. Any or all of these aspects of a place might be represented in either a sketch map or a GIS product.

In teacher research with adolescents, I found the role of social value highly evident in the analysis of student sketch maps. In this, I see parallels with research in sociolinguisitc ethnography. Sociolinguistic studies have yielded influences of social context upon language acquisition, competence, performance, and literacy. Since all learning is situated within these influences, we can assess their impact on what students choose to retain. What is selected to remain "in" or "out" of a sketch is influenced greatly by cultural values.

Downs and Stea (1977) identified (1) functional importance and (2) distinctiveness or imagability as the primary factors influencing the selection of data represented. Both are rooted in sociocultural values. For example, in English usage, "wastes" or spaces not necessarily occupied by a recognizable "use" would not appear in a sketch map simply because there is a lesser social value attached to those places than there is, for example, to a shopping mall.

Applying a Functionalist Perspective

From Downs and Stea's "functional importance" (as determined by social value), let us begin to compare spatial and linguistic products. In the following section, I discuss the distinctiveness of those products. With respect to the map, its functional properties to the reader are many, but let us first classify it as what psychologist Lynn Liben called a "spatial product." For Liben (1981), a spatial product is "any map, model, or verbal description."

The Spatial Domain

Humans must often maneuver in new environments, must integrate prior spatial knowledge with unfamiliar environmental inputs (terrestrial, atmospheric, celestial), and must constantly interpret the spatial behaviors of others (human, animal) in order to make decisions in real time. The responses required in these decisions take place within environmental settings, aided by mental representations of the settings. In other words, we are always trying to interpret from multiple frames, "What's going on here?" The decisions made will determine possible courses of action that may require or demonstrate an individual's competence.

Still considered a central resource in understanding the related human spatial functions is Liben, Patterson, and Newcombe's *Spatial Representation and Behavior Across the Lifespan* (1981). In her introduction, Liben proposes a typology of spatial representations both internal and external. Her types are as follows:

1. *Spatial storage,* which refers to spatial information about space stored "in one's head." This information may be stored as truth propositions, pure relations, stimulus-response bonds, or imagistic format, isolated or integrated. The individual is not cognizant of this stored information; once the individual becomes cognizant of it, it becomes spatial thought.

2. *Spatial thought,* which refers to thinking that makes use of space in some way. Individuals have access to, can reflect upon, or can manipulate spatial thought in spatial problem solving or imagery. This would include such operations as mental rotation (the ability to alter one's

perspective of an image mentally), as well as many other mental image transformations.

3. *Spatial products,* which refers to external representations of space such as sketch maps, models, and verbal descriptions (I interpret this to include written descriptions as well).

The Liben volume also describes numerous spatial behavioral operations and cognitive processes. According to Liben's typology, a map is a spatial product; it is an external representation. My aim here is to locate maps as products within a broad range of spatial behaviors comparable to linguistic products from a broad range of linguistic behaviors. In the above, *stored* linguistic "lexical items" might be words; *thought* would be the sequencing of words (or syntax) to represent meaning (semantics); and the *product* would be the sentence, spoken or typed.

● The GIS Connection

The GIS Connection: the features, functions, and buttons of a GIS can exemplify Liben's typology. Items found in spatial storage would relate to the various databases, maps, and images that could reside in a GIS project. These are known as themes, tables, and attributes. These are brought together through activating GIS *functions,* which relate to spatial thought, in which the items in storage could be manipulated on the computer in the GIS. Finally, the outcome of one's spatial thought and manipulation would be a map or spatial product. See the Chapter 2 GIS Connection: "Buttons, Functions, and Features."

Students Making Spatial Meaning

During early adolescence, children of many cultures begin to explore their environs more widely. Here, opportunities to explore unknown areas, to get lost and find their way again, and to negotiate new routes allow adolescents to practice independent wayfinding. The cultural expectation is one of spatial competence. In schools, students are expected to find their way to various classrooms and activities within complex buildings and schedules.

By late adolescence, in Western cultures, many adolescents are learning to drive, combining what could be considered a set of spatial competencies. In other cultures, spatial competencies might differ entirely. Adolescent females in subsistence agricultural societies might be living in a different household, expected to forage, farm, work in a city, or to remain within a relatively small range from the home. Males might be expected to practice pastoral nomadism far from the home village, sometimes completely isolated. Others might be responsible for cultivating sizable properties.

This indulgence of descriptions of spatial behaviors and competencies is my effort to make them "visible," because in Western culture and academic biases, these competencies are not valued, recognized, or developed in schools, even when the Western economy is based upon spatial design and representation of new products. A limited recognition of spatial competence appears in the sports arena, where "points scored" become the focus rather than the spatial competencies required to have made the scored points possible. The traditional industrial arts curriculum is another area where spatial intelligence is required and developed, but this part of the curriculum is sadly not as highly valued, nor is it widely enough recognized as a place where architects and engineers are taught and discover their own talents.

By integrating the prior spatial knowledge adolescents possess about the world and applying that knowledge to new knowledge and problems, a more substantial link between actual experience and abstract concepts might be facilitated. If discussions of adolescents' spatial experiences and competencies are conducted, the level of "metaspatial cognition," analogous to the concept of "metalinguistic cogntion," becomes articulated or visible. In reading and writing education, particular attention is focused on eliciting metalinguistic cognition as a way to bring learners toward the linguistic competencies of reading and writing. In these settings, students are encouraged to talk about their writing strategies. In teacher research, I used this metacognitive approach with students assessing their own learning using sketch maps. In the next section, I describe teacher research I did with students between 1990 and 1994. If "a picture is worth a thousand words," the students' sketch maps should help to tell the story.

Social and Spatial Context of Learner/Participants

Using the highly discrete region of Cape Cod, a peninsula in southeastern Massachusetts, as a subject of study with ninth-grade students roughly fourteen years old, not yet drivers, the "before" mental maps (Figure 2–2) were predictably sketchy. To put the ninth graders into social and spatial context, it was the students' first day attending a twelve-town regional high school. The legal driving age is sixteen and a half, so most had not mastered this culturally significant skill and rite of passage. Neither had they been required to produce map representations for that purpose, as culturally, the expectation of a freshman is simply that he or she will ride the bus.

The sketch map–artifacts by students in this age group were generally constituted of three basic components: (1) an outline of the rough shape of the peninsular landform, (2) the labeling of terminus points (the Cape Cod Canal and Provincetown), and (3) the student's home community, centered within the region. These provide us with the "edges" and landmarks ("nodes") described by

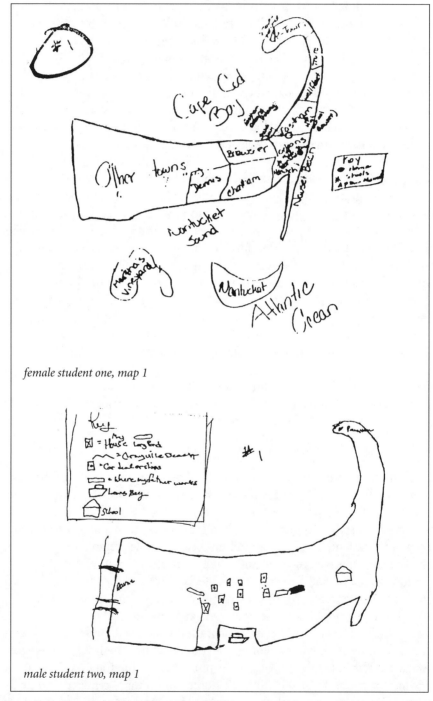

female student one, map 1

male student two, map 1

Figure 2–2. *Cape Cod Map 1 (September 1989)*

Lynch (1960), and the centrism (Saarinen 1988) and relative location (GENIP 1987) of the home community.

Some students attempted to locate the relative positions of the school, the shopping mall, or other personally or culturally significant landmarks. Others took artistic license, adding symbols of fish, whales, boats, or other recreational landmarks in a fashion similar to those of historic cartographers' maps, where the relative sizes of such cultural features are greatly augmented. As artifacts, these products can yield information about the strategies of constructive cognitive spatial processing, especially when compared to the students' "after" versions of the regional map.

Intervention

Between their production of Map 1 and Map 2, students participated in a two-week unit of study on the Cape Cod region. The basic outline of the unit was:

Week 1: The Glacial Period

The Wisconsin glacier in North America

Glacial deposition and the geology of Cape Cod

> Situating the formation of the Cape in time and space

Week 2: Glacial formations of landforms and water bodies of Cape Cod

Processes of deposition and erosion

Moraines

Outwash plains

Kame and kettle landscapes

Barrier beach ("spit") formations

Political units (towns)

In Week 1 of the unit, the Cape landform was first situated as a consequence of the Wisconsin Glacial Period. Students mapped the extent of the glacier over the North American continent. The impacts and movements (concepts: processes of weathering and erosion) were studied and students constructed diagrams of glacial phenomena.

In Week 2, these phenomena were related to the local landforms and water bodies of Cape Cod with which students were familiar, using materials prepared by the U.S. Geological Survey and the Cape Cod National Seashore to reinforce students' experience in Cape Cod landscapes, and to enhance pattern recognition in conjunction with familiar place-name associations.

Students mapped these features in conjunction with map key and shading techniques. While they were mapping the landform, I asked students to visualize certain locations on the Mid-Cape highway with which they might have been familiar to connect the task with any prior knowledge they had in the form of mental imagery, mentioning specific vistas, bridges, and landmarks.

After the layer of geological landform information had been completed, the layer of political information was added to student maps. The town boundaries were printed on the map, while the students delineated the geologic landform information. They therefore were not required to draw in the town lines, but simply to label the towns. Selected familiar National Seashore and conservation/recreation areas were also located and labeled.

After the regional study, when the second set of mental maps was drawn, students demonstrated greater articulation of detail in the shape of the landform. More information had also been added *within* the map about spatial relationships and political boundaries of towns and their relative and proximal locations. This had implications for both the students and me regarding learning strategies; we discovered that learned information is fit into an existing mental framework articulated from a general outline to a more distinct specific representation (see Figure 2–3).

While the concept of general-to-specific isn't news to the educational community, it does point to what became for me a dependable sequence for instruction. That is, I began to frame the teaching of social studies in a spatial context for my particular learners, and although they were somewhat unique in being technical school students, I have found this framework useful at all educational levels. I had also extrapolated what I had learned about engaging hands-on or spatial activities across my teaching. The entire educational genre of graphic organizers is grounded in this approach, and much reading and literacy research supports that imageability enhances reading comprehension and retention.

The process/product relationship becomes clarified in light of this analysis of the student maps as artifacts. Here the student can view his/her own process and progress as reflected in the difference between the "before" and "after" products. This reveals another educational purpose for using sketch mapping; that of its utility in developing metacognitive processing. As the learner compares her first artifact with her most recent, spatial knowledge acquisition processes in her own spatial relations can be reflected in the representations. A teacher might ask questions to stimulate metacognitive awareness of identifiable strategies in spatial processing, or address misconceptions if necessary.

Additional elements appearing in the second representation show influences of formal curriculum, cultural context, and social and personal agenda. On the second set of student maps, political units had become more

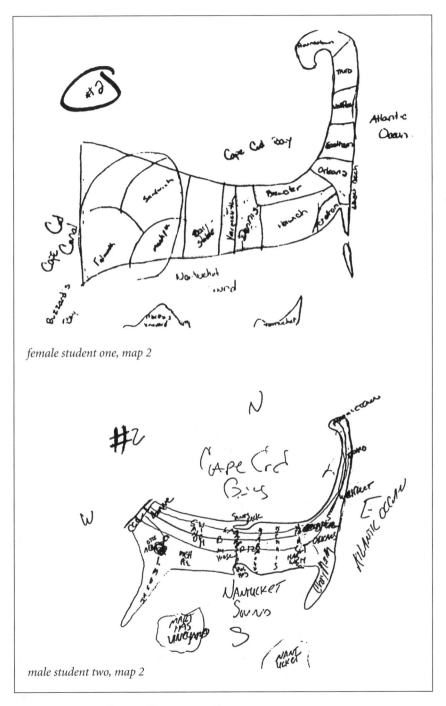

female student one, map 2

male student two, map 2

Figure 2–3. *Cape Cod Map 2 (January 1990)*

distinctly articulated, but physical features and water bodies were still unclear, although they had been studied and mapped. This may indicate students' priorities on town locations.

Adolescents' Learning as Situated in Social Context

In the minds and experiences of my student mapmakers, newly identified political units—towns—may by this time have become imbued with the social significance or meaning of new school friends hailing from different towns. Or they may have been thought to have future social-functional value for these American teens for whom driving was the upcoming rite of passage, and for whom mastery of direction and travel would indicate social competence.

It is this sense of social value, significance, or meaning that begs the use of an analysis that could parallel a sociolinguistic analysis. Sociolinguist-ethnographers have undertaken the process of identifying and locating influences of social context upon language acquisition and competence. This context, and the values both explicit and implicit therein, mediate individual learners' goals for language acquisition, competency, and literacy. By mediated, I mean the cultural filter through which "what I need to know and be able to do" is first, culturally learned, second, seen (or "instantiated"), and third, reproduced. Therefore, if the society values the competency of driving, it will be held as a value or by the initiates, therefore seen as a valuable competency, and again reproduced to demonstrate competency as an adult member of the society (compare this to the aging neighbor's onset inability to drive). In the U.S., it is among the sacred rites of passage. These values, then, would parallel the functions of spatial knowledge acquisition, competence, and literacy. These functions have been long established in the literature of sociolinguistics and learning, competence, and literacy.

As we investigate learners' understanding of spatial operations, it can be useful to analyze spatial skills and their acquisition, competency, and literacy. In other words, what is the *social* or cultural value on learning, successfully using, or retaining spatial information? How do social roles, specifically gender and socioeconomic, influence the premiums placed on spatial competence? At which spatial tasks is one expected to be competent?

In an audiotaped group interview with a sample of these adolescent mapmakers, a sudden and reverent hush fell over their normally animated conversation when asked the question, "What does it mean to get a driver's license?" After a distinctly pregnant pause, one student replied, "It's everything!" Another said, "It's freedom. It means you don't have to ask your mother every time you want to go somewhere."

Teachers of adolescents anywhere in North America would recognize this response as simply basic to that age group, but it is yet one more of those invisible, implicit assumptions about spatial competence that is so embedded in our culture that we don't recognize its importance or significance—we simply assume it. We certainly provide driver's education as part of the curriculum, yet the test is almost strictly performance-based (most states have a cursory ten-question written or computer-based test as part of the licensing process). Yet here, we give license to adolescents to commandeer an expensive, powerful, and potentially dangerous vehicle, the successful operation of which has immense social significance and responsibility.

Let's examine the students' use of the word *somewhere*. It appears, at very least, that the extent of "somewhere" has certainly expanded to an area no longer considered attainable (or socially acceptably attainable) by bicycle. The cultural value of the "freedom" associated with licensure is clearly a rite of passage, but in terms of spatial competence, this also has implications. The licensee will now have access to, but *must master the competencies inherent in,* what many have described as a "car culture." This change in spatial performance and competence expectations was reflected in Cape Cod Map 3 (Figure 2–4), which was produced two years after Map 2, and after the participants had been driving.

By the time these mappers were in grade 12, their maps included the east-west axis highways that connect the towns of the region. Given their weekly attendance at a regional school, an interesting comparative study with similar-aged students attending hometown schools might yield varying results. In any case, to these adolescents, an expectation of spatial competence was constituted by successful navigation in driving and wayfinding. This brings us back to a discussion of the mental map as a representational product (or output) of spatial competence and literacy.

While I had devoted fairly heavy instructional time to students' actually drawing maps of the glacial moraine and outwash plain areas on student maps of Cape Cod, when they produced their second sketch maps, what they had retained were the locations of the towns. This is what was important to *them*. Given further assessments that tested their understanding of moraines and outwash plains—on linguistic-based tests—they were able to demonstrate competence, but there were clearly two different agendas here. Again, the differentiation of learning targets between teachers and learners is not news; it is simply significant that, asked to map Cape Cod, the selection of socially significant (political) features was what they chose to represent, not the geological nature of our unit of study.

After reflecting on this (as we teachers are encouraged to do), I have concluded that there are social and cultural expectations brought to the task of "drawing your map" of a place, and that those expectations reveal our implicit expectations of competence. What is left now is to understand more

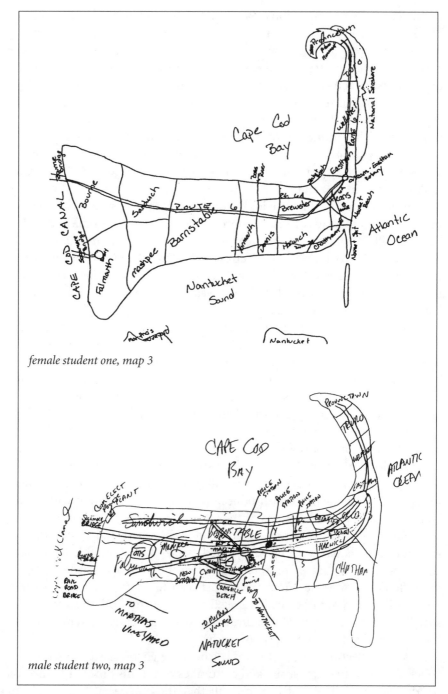

Figure 2–4. *Cape Cod Map 3 (June 1992)*

fully how to further articulate the many spatial competencies we implicitly (invisibly) expect and perform, and integrate them into learning and teaching with spatial intelligence, cognition, and competency in mind.

A Functionalist Comparison

In function, the domain of "language" covers a much wider range of communication than does that of a map. A more congruent range is to compare language with spatial behavior. To address the need for a spatial representation of the comparative domains and corresponding functions of linguistic and spatial behavior and communication, I have tried to compare them in a graphic organizer (see Figure 2–5).

While to the reader the functional properties of a map are many, I return to what psychologist Liben calls a "spatial product." For Liben, a spatial product is "any map, model, or verbal description" (1981). For the sake of this comparison, let us also take verbal to include written descriptions. The map's counterpart in the linguistic domain would also be a product.

There are several literary forms with functions similar to those of map products. These literary products, such as land titles, guidebooks, scientific or geographic treatises, histories, and certain novels, all have functions parallel to different types of maps. None of these genres are exactly congruent, but to the degree that any genre is delimited in that it does not duplicate another, we can assert that certain literary forms parallel the functions of certain map forms.

In Figure 2–5, I have represented only two of Howard Gardner's multiple intelligences: linguistic and spatial intelligence. These were selected for the purpose of this comparison. Using Gardner's theory, I would expect to find parallel functions across the full range of intelligences.

Once we've seen the comparative functions within the realms of linguistic and spatial intelligence, how do we go about teaching to or for them?

First, simply identifying parallel functions for both ourselves and students can be helpful. Second, once process-product relationships are drawn, students might select one or more modes of representation to meet a particular task. Third, the utility of compared functions may lead to comparisons across the remaining intelligences, using what Gardner calls symbolic representation, to reveal genres and more options for student success. It is through this understanding that gender gaps might be more easily bridged.

In Summary

In this chapter, we've looked at the shifting foci of social studies as reflective of twentieth-century culture. Although technological advances have forged new

< ~~~~~~~~~~~~~~~~~~~~~~~~"MIND" ~~~~~~~~~~~~~~~~~~~~~~~~~>

Cognitive processes

(Liben's "spatial storage")

<- - - *Pattern Recognition* - - ->

< ~ **LINGUISTIC** ~~~ (spectrum of Gardner's "intelligences") ~~~ **SPATIAL** ~ >

```
                              /      (Liben's "spatial thought")        S
L                             \                                         p
         Phoneme recognition      (SOUND)         Echolocation          a
A                             \                                         t
                                                                        i
N             COMMUNICATIVE BEHAVIORS                                   a
         Nonverbal sounds         /      Gestures/direction of movement l
                              \
G (Pinker's "Proto-speech") ~ SYMBOLIC COMMUNICATION ~ (E. Hall's Proxemics)
                                                                        B
U                        Competencies                                  e
   Comprehensible input/output  \  Successful locomotion, operations in space  h
A           Conversation         /      Wayfinding, site selection     a
         Logical argument        \   Arrange/design work & living spaces  v
G         Public speaking        /  Mastering transportation routes, driving, etc.  i
             Literacy            \          Map reading                 o
E                                /                                      r
```

Products of Comparable Function

```
                                 \      (Liben's "Spatial Products")
        Verbal directions         /        Hand-drawn street map
   Travelogue, written geography  \  Landscape, scene, photo, oblique map
         Property deed            /      Parcel map, surveyor's plan
                                 \
                                  /
```

< ~ **LINGUISTIC** ~~~ (spectrum of Gardner's "intelligences") ~~~ SPATIAL ~ >

Figure 2–5. *A Functional Model for Comparing Spatial and Linguistic Cognition*
Beginning within the broad concept of "mind," communicative behaviors considered linguistic and spatial are listed by comparative function and clustered near either "intelligence" along a continuum. From the communicative behaviors, competencies and products also develop. Many other behaviors could be added in either category, or under different types of "intelligence" along an expanded continuum. Notice that as subcategories of communicative behavior "funnel down" toward products, functional comparisons become more closely related.

understandings and dimensions of human activity, the centrifugal nationalistic forces manifesting in crumbling political states cannot be ignored. While education is certainly part of the solution, the spatial problems of ever higher human population will not go away. These will be the continuing issues and problems of this century; the question is, will we have learned from history and from the successful problem solving we have managed to establish?

One thing we've learned is that this is it—this planet is home. There are fewer illusions about colonizing space, at least for the foreseeable future. While some political nations have reached the realization that Mutual Armed Destruction is completely suicidal, other entities seek the weapons that would portend that end. These are the peoples who haven't been afforded expression in a democratic forum. And unless we train students in those practices, they may retreat from democratic participation as well. The practice of democracy cannot become part of the forbidden curriculum.

Through teacher research, I found understandings of student spatial behavior, learning, cognition, and problem solving, and how they are situated within a cultural context. I applied a functionalist perspective to compare the processes and products of spatial and linguistic behavior, cognition, and intelligence to better balance learning activities in the classroom.

The implications are that we need to learn more about what constitutes spatial competence—what are the skills students have or don't have? We barely have insight into this, yet we know that video and computer games exploit those same proclivities.

How does GIS fit into this part of the equation? In many ways, GIS is a technology that can put students' spatial skills to significant learning tasks and opportunities in social studies. No longer able to remain complacent about global issues, and in an effort to recommit ourselves as leaders in social studies, we can incorporate and enrich both local and global understandings using GIS.

As Haque reminds us, GIS must be seen and used as a tool of democracy, empowerment, and equity. I believe that the best frame from which GIS can be integrated is through NCSS's theme of science, technology, and society (STS). Unexamined, GIS technocrats can create a mapped world that excludes rather than includes, obfuscates rather than illustrates, and perpetrates rather than emancipates. The onus, as we shall see in Chapter 4, is upon public participation for democratization, preservation, and conservation. GIS will either be a tool of domination or participation.

From here, we will see examples of classroom GIS integration and a discussion of an ideal setting for the inclusion of GIS in conducting social studies. In the chapters that follow, I present examples of schools in which this active participation was facilitated through projects integrating GIS. Those schools were every bit as lively as and as hampered by state and national standards as any other school in the U.S., but the teachers took risks far more demanding than the skill or computer power needed now to integrate GIS. Let's look into those classrooms and see what can happen!

3

Where Is GIS in Schools and in Social Studies?

Why Include GIS in Social Studies Classrooms?

It is essential that we continue to teach concepts of geography in social studies. An understanding of spatial and cultural issues is central to geography and, it would appear, to our shared future. As we continue to populate this planet with unprecedented numbers of humans, we will face not fewer, but more conflicts over space, resources, distribution of resources, and power over resources.

How will today's students best be the problem solvers of the twenty-first century? Is it in their (and our) best interests to consciously avoid the knowledge of spatial and geographic issues and problems? Because if we do not address these in social studies classrooms, we have, by default or deselection, decided not to prepare students for the world they will inherit, must understand, and must work together to construct.

By including this tool of geographic representation, we create the possibility that today's students will be prepared with layered understandings of space, history, culture, and environment, all essential to the survival of the species. Perhaps more imperative is the presentation of geographic understandings and GIS in a context of social studies and its themes applying critical perspectives and ethical practice for sustainable communities.

To do anything less is to deny the future and the fact that there will be inherent social, geopolitical, and economic problems; to deny that technology cannot in and of itself solve everything; and to deny the shifting role of educators in that future. In some cases it may mean that teachers must make conscious choices in their students' preparation. Are they preparing students for their futures or are they preparing them for a test?

Social studies teachers have always had to balance these issues within their practice. The inclusion of geography and/or GIS also means that many teachers will have to educate themselves. We hope that this book will be a bridge toward that shared future of problem solving and cultural and environmental understanding.

How Is GIS Currently Used in Conducting Social Studies?

A great place to see how teachers and students are integrating GIS is through ESRI's extensive schools and libraries website, <www.esri.com/k-12>. Arguably the single most-visited website by K–12 educators integrating GIS, the site is maintained, updated, and linked to support from ESRI's schools and libraries team, Charlie Fitzpatrick, George Dailey, and Angela Lee. Among other resources found at the site are lessons using ArcView, at <www.esri.com/arclessons>, and downloadable ArcVoyager software (graciously provided for you on the CD in the back of this book by agreement with ESRI). Put the book down and go exploring on the website. While you're there, go to the ESRI home page at <www.esri.com> and look for online demos from the index on the left side of the page. This is a great site for students to begin building an understanding of what GIS can do. This is where we start with university students to discover some of the many utilities of GIS.

The GIS Connection

In this section, I describe several Internet and teacher-developed projects that may be found on the CD. These can help connect GIS to your classroom. For a total immersion into conducting social studies with GIS, visit the Community Atlas Project at <www.esri.com/communityatlas>. With this project, a school can begin to develop a profile of its community using data available online from a variety of resources. As a first step, set a few technology-savvy students onto the community atlas project to begin developing a student base and an information base to which other investigations could connect. Featured on the website is Lynn Malone of Great Barrington, Rhode Island. Lynn began integrating GIS this way and has ongoing community GIS projects as part of her middle school geography classes.

Introduced for 2002 is the international project at <www.geography.com/sustainable> that invites participants from the global community to contribute projects to a central location.

At ESRI's 2001 ESRI EdUC (Educators' User Conference), <www.esri.com/gisedconf>, Carl C. Addington presented a Civil War history project entitled "The Killer Angels: A GIS of the Battle of Gettysburg, July 1–3, 1863" that traced battalion movements in the battles depicted in the film *Gettysburg*. Addington presented *Gettysburg* and GIS maps he developed to enhance his students' understanding of the terrain and the locations of the battles, distributing a companion CD to the film.

In a similar project, Christopher Harris, working with fifth-grade students, followed the trail of a particular regiment that hailed from the students' home state of North Carolina. Developer Harris described his project, "Footsteps of Glory: Using GIS to Track the North Carolina 26th Regiment," this way:

> I worked with fifth-grade students to locate Civil War battles in which the NC 26th played an important role. We then located these battles in a GIS map and used PowerPoint to create a "movie" of the troop movements. The troop statistics from the battles were used in math as we studied ratios and percentages.
>
> This project, the teacher told me, brought out more excitement and dedication to work than he has seen in many years. Students connected with the spatial representations offered by GIS, and were drawn into the stories that surfaced when we probed the documents and history of the regiment. We titled the project in honor of the men who advanced the furthest of all the soldiers in Pickett's Charge while suffering great losses.

A short PowerPoint of Chris' project is included on the companion CD to this book.

In Chapter 5, I describe in greater detail an African American Civil Rights–era history project conducted in a middle school that included 125 middle school students, some who conducted oral history interviews, and some who developed GIS maps from geographic references (or "georeferences") in the interviews and archival photos that depicted pre- and Civil Rights–era Raleigh. As students interviewed the alumni of their middle school, which had been a historically black high school, they learned about the history of their community in a new way and became the recorders of that history.

This was a service to a community that might never have afforded the human power to conduct this type of project. Thus, the students became historians of the African American experience in Civil Rights–era Raleigh, literally putting that experience "on the map." An extensive website illustrates many of the project's products: <www2.ncsu.edu/ncsu/cep/ligon/about/history/esri/P7311.htm>.

In a recent semester of our GIS in Education course, projects ranged from elementary- to graduate-level projects. Harris' and the next three examples are based on the work of inservice teachers who participated in a GIS in Education course. Two of the elementary projects were investigations of local history.

Barbaree Ash Duke, in working with third-grade students, began from a local history book, *Both Sides of the Tracks: A Profile of the Colored Community of Cary, NC* (1996), by Ella Arrington Williams-Vinson, about the town of Cary, North Carolina. The Cary described is vastly different from the Cary of today, and Duke wanted to illustrate to her young students how the changes had occurred. She contacted Cary's GIS department, where she was given digital base maps of the parts of town developed over the past century. As Duke read the book with her students, she displayed the maps, locating the school and other landmarks in the town. By switching on the street layer, students could find their own neighborhoods and evaluate in which periods various parts of town had developed. This can help to develop that layered historic understanding of their community and place over time, with themselves included in it.

Another third-grade teacher, Cheryl Davis, took the idea of Barbaree's project a step further; she was interested in the controversial school districting issue. As she began to investigate the process used in her county to locate new schools and designate their contributing geographic areas, she began to influence the county GIS office in how they were approaching the problem! Unable to complete that (hugely ambitious) project, she began instead to research designated historic features listed in a database. Again, Cheryl found incomplete data, but the list seemed promising—its points could be located on the county street map, so she began doing what's known as a "windshield assessment" of the locations.

Driving through her community, looking for the designated features, Cheryl located some historic sites—buildings, chapels, and cemeteries—that began to enrich her historical understanding of the community. She photographed these and hotlinked the photos to the designated sites on her digital map. As a community history project, linked directly to the North Carolina third-grade social studies curriculum, the project combined several of her own interests as it integrated an appropriate technology (see Figure 3–1).

About her "Our School District's History" project, National Board certified teacher Cheryl Davis says:

> Younger students may not have the computer skills to do GIS projects independently, but they are very capable of using GIS to enhance learning. Activities can be teacher-led, or a few students can be taught the necessary skills, and become group leaders for cooperative learning activities. Prior experience with various types of globes and maps is also helpful.
>
> Integrating GIS with social studies is a wonderful way to make map studies come alive providing opportunities to develop critical thinking skills. My GIS project focused on our own community—our school district. Students used the maps to compare how our school district has

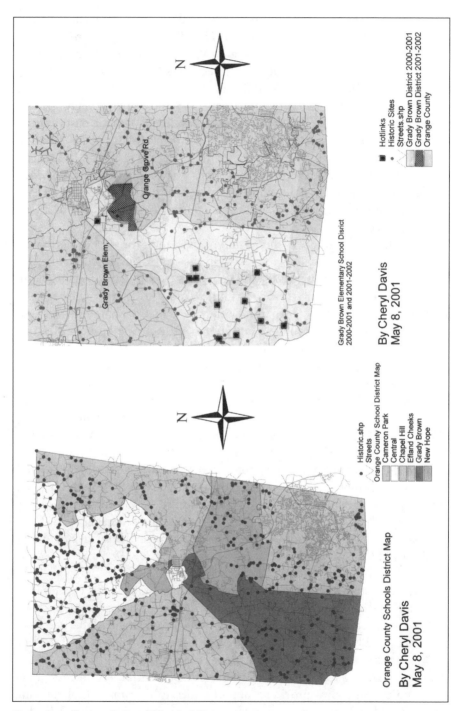

Figure 3–1. *Orange County Historical Sites*

changed over time. They can use these maps to research historical sites close to our school. Hotlinked photos provide an historic record of the sites; students can take virtual field trips of the sites following the streets shown on the map.

At first I had trouble finding local data, but connecting with a community GIS specialist was the key. After some legwork, I located some large paper maps, which the GIS office digitized. I got what I wanted, and so did they! This project can now be used with not just this year's students but will be ready for future classes. After all, our community is constantly changing!

In an interdisciplinary middle school project, teacher Nancy Hook developed a "Techno Book Review" incorporating GIS. Nancy describes the project this way:

This interdisciplinary project incorporates GIS mapping and is adaptable to a variety of content areas and learning styles. How does it work? Students begin by reading an age-appropriate book based on a journey. Students map the character's journey, adding relevant math-related data. ArcView (GIS) software extends student learning through visually representing spatial relationships. Finally, students create GIS layouts with graphs and hotlinks, sharing their books with other students using PowerPoint. Reading *Walkabout*, one student mapped the downed plane crash and journey, made a map of Aboriginal culture, and graphed rainfall statistics important to the story.

An example of the "Techno Book Review" can be found on the companion CD.

In the Watts area of Los Angeles, high school teacher Herschel Sarnoff has been working since 1998 to integrate GIS into social studies classes. Sarnoff has developed history-based GIS lessons hosted on ESRI's ArcLessons website, <www.esri.com/arclessons>. Sarnoff's "Census 1790: Slaves as Percent of U.S. Population in Each State" project is available on the Web at: <www.tcla.gseis.ucla.edu/divide/teachers/lausd_jordan.html>. At that site, Herschel tells the story of his introduction to GIS and ways that he and his students have incorporated it into a variety of courses. A number of their studies are posted on the Web, and his work with students is described in greater depth in Chapter 7.

The Look of an Ideal Classroom for Conducting Social Studies

To my delight and joy, I was asked by a former social studies methods student, now an incredibly resourceful and active teacher and coach, to come and do a GIS presentation in her high school elective geography class. What a treat! Rebecca Bradford had designed what all of us would hope to create as a flexible and responsive learning and teaching environment. Her class was large—thirty students—and bear in mind that all had elected to be there. Happily it was free of required end-of-course testing, so there could be an atmosphere of learning for the fun of it, or the joy of it! The class enjoyed the following advantages:

First, the course was held in a block schedule, so we could move from one type of activity to another without losing a lot of "time off task."

Second, there were three computers in the classroom; two desktops (one connected to the Internet) and one laptop on the teacher's desk that could be used to project to the front of the room from a mobile cart.

Third, the phone line allowed Rebecca telephone and Internet access.

Fourth, adjacent through a side door in her classroom was a shared computer lab for which Rebecca was the responsible faculty member. This allowed us to move into the lab without passing through hallways, and students could search on websites I'd provided to find GIS resources such as online mapping, aerial and satellite imagery, and other GIS-related sources.

Fifth, Rebecca borrowed an LCD projector that we could hook up to my laptop (though we could have used her school-purchased laptop).

Sixth was a resource I think is fabulous, a dedicated student assistant, whom I asked to locate certain Web resources on GIS jobs and an animated version of continental drift. He was able, during my introductory session, to find and demonstrate the two sites. What a tremendous resource for teachers! And what an important opportunity for the students! Many schools now have programs of in-house teaching assistants—an absolutely essential idea, for the reasons I mentioned in Chapter 1. Here is a way that students can become agents and contributing members of the community as they learn to conduct social studies!

Had the computer lab also had a networked projector, any of the students could have displayed their findings from the search to the rest of the class on a large screen. When we moved into the lab, I gave pairs of students a list of websites that offer GIS online (see the Resources section). They explored the sites and shared their explorations with the class.

Rebecca had several student products displayed; there was evidence of lots of hands-on original student construction of different types—masks, weavings, relief maps, replicas of cultural artifacts. Rebecca mentioned some three different guest speakers who had visited the class over the course of the semester—facilitated by the telephone access, without a doubt.

I should point out that Rebecca's school, Fuquay-Varina High School in Wake County, North Carolina, isn't a new school, but resources have been used wisely, and by volunteering to manage the computer lab, Rebecca has earned access to it. She sought out the student assistants for her three block classes, she designed the activities that interested students enough to take her geography class and to pass on the word that it was a great elective. So the facilities are part of it, but certainly not all of it! Rebecca sees the world as her classroom and has garnered the necessary tools for putting that philosophy into practice!

GIS Inside the Schools and Outside in the Communities

In Rebecca's classroom, we saw how a student assistant was an integral player. Any instructor who's trying to integrate technology knows from experience that students' skills vary widely, but that usually there will be one or two students whose computer skills are an immense resource. If that teacher is at all resourceful, he or she will already have asked those students to assist in teaching not only other students, but also the teacher him- or herself, some of the tricks of the technology.

The contribution of those students is immeasurable, and Harvard's Christopher Dede has written about "technology-enabled learning environments" as places where there is what's called distributed collaborative learning and teaching (2000). Okay, what does that mean? Well, it means that we must acknowledge that the workplaces in which our current students will work won't resemble the environments of the past, where isolated workers pushed paper and typed out reports in a vacuum. Neither do our classrooms model the future landscapes of productivity in the postindustrial, postmodern world.

While there is still paper being pushed, to be sure, much of it has been replaced by electronic transfers, messages, and files. One of the major differences is that one is no longer "virtually" isolated. Communications technologies have changed all that. (Who among us hasn't cursed email at least a few times a month?) With every new email comes another request for service, another inquiry, another possibility. The electronic communications represent the "distributed" part of the educational jargon. But the collaborative components may be either actual or virtual. In projects I've visited and directed, I prefer that the collaborative part be in the actual domain. Collaboration with community partners, other teachers, or other students is a most effective way to engage the synergistic thinking required for conducting social studies. Experiencing the "Yeah, that's cool!—and then we could . . ." synergy of learning together is a goal state for students' minds.

Current classrooms don't reflect much of how we should prepare students to operate in their futures. Neglecting the distributed nature of information and collaboration that are becoming increasingly part of the workplace environment means that students are still learning in an obsolete model. While GIS in and of itself doesn't change that, its nature as a software used to synthesize and analyze Internet-borne information for local and regional problem solving makes it an important technology of choice for transforming classrooms, schools, and communities. We are also finding that integrating GIS expands the classroom to incorporate community technical assistance and establishes new horizons for participation by and among students, teachers, and their communities.

If communities can be seen as energy, and students are seen as vital sources of that energy, how can schools be seen as conduits for that energy? Since working with GIS, our views of technology in education have changed in that technology should *serve* education, and education should serve the community. By this we mean not just in educating students, but in providing services directly *to* the community toward its and therefore the school's sustainability. In reconceptualizing GIS in education, we are now back to recognizing the critical link of social studies with communities and GIS as an active link in that process. The nature of GIS technology literally helps facilitate collaborative relationships (see Figure 3–2). Our views on this have been reaffirmed by social and political events of this turn-of-the-century period.

How Do Secondary Students View Themselves in Their Communities?

When we posed this question to a random group of high school students, we were sometimes shocked, often dismayed, and occasionally warmed by what we saw. In an unpublished study, we asked some 140 students to "draw a representation of yourself in your community" and developed some criteria for interpretation, drew some preliminary conclusions, and were left with more questions than answers. Less than a fifth of the students represented their worlds as focused on school. Many drew buildings, blocks, or neighborhoods. Others drew haunting images of lonely lives spent indoors, isolated from their communities. Others showed themselves in community service, with friends, or with family. Less than a fifth of the students represented themselves taking an active role in the community through community service (8 percent); work (8 percent); recycling (4 percent); removing trash and other chores (4 percent). After viewing these samples, I wanted to investigate how the same task by students learning with GIS might compare with those of the control group.

Students as Agents

In Rebecca's and Herschel's classrooms, we saw students taking active roles in technology integration. As we look into the schools in chapters 4–9, we'll be seeing fundamentally different roles taken by students. In these settings, we'll

Figure 3–2. *Student Representation: "What Community? I Don't Have a Community"*

see *students as agents*, working collaboratively both with one another and with their teachers to coconstruct their learning environments. This represents a shift in the social structure of the classroom. We will be seeing more of this in the participating schools.

The Participating Schools

The schools I visited had been experimenting with GIS early on (meaning from 1994). Most of the projects have evolved or the teachers have moved on, retired, or have taken on new dimensions of furthering GIS in education. Only one of the ten has retired from GIS integration; most are exploring new applications.

In these schools, students took very active roles, sharing decision making with the teachers and with one another. These settings were sociologically different from traditional social studies classrooms that aren't engaged in original inquiry or research. The teachers in these schools speak in the following chapters about depending upon and trusting students to explore and manipulate the GIS software on their own; to co-instruct their peers and their teachers. The teachers described this as liberating to them and as essential to the integration of the technology.

During the period these teachers were pioneering GIS use, the software was undergoing transition from a DOS-based application to a Windows-based format, adding mouse utility and greater facility. Since then, ArcVoyager, which appears on our companion CD, was developed by ESRI's Charlie Fitzpatrick, a former geography teacher. Charlie essentially embodies the GIS-in-education movement, and now has two colleagues within ESRI who share the expanding demand for developments in GIS educational applications.

Once the Internet became an integral force in education, as it already had in research and in GIS, ESRI's School GIS website (<www.esri.com/k-12>) became perhaps the single most important hub for GIS in education. If you haven't visited it yet, put down this book and navigate to it! Come back to the stories of the schools once you've visited that site.

Okay, now that you're back, I want to introduce the five schools we'll be visiting in the next five chapters. Students learning with GIS could not be randomly selected as too few schools had or have sufficiently developed programs using GIS to yield adequate random sampling. So few schools have enrollments of over fifty students per year in GIS courses that the students, teachers, and communities I describe must be viewed from this necessarily small sample. I have used ethnographic case study research as my method of inquiry.

Pseudonyms have been used for each school, student, and teacher as permissions for research prescribed. Students were randomly selected from classes involved in GIS teaching and learning. In three of the situations, I interviewed students in the classroom as class went on around us. This is indicative of the type of inquiry found in GIS classrooms: students were involved in projects; teachers gave introductory comments and directions, and then students worked, usually in teams, on specific projects using GIS as an analytical tool. None were traditional teacher-lecture-type classrooms.

In the following pages, I briefly introduce five schools in which GIS was included in instruction or in a community project. I briefly describe the school and community context of the GIS teaching and learning, and touch upon the community relationships. All of these themes are expanded upon in the following chapters. After each of the interviews, I asked each student, "Would you please draw a representation of yourself in your community?" Selected representations appear in the introductions below.

Baymouth High School (Chapter 4)

Our first school, which I call Baymouth, is located in a seaside community in Massachusetts. The project was an afterschool environmental community service project. Baymouth is the only public high school in a sixty-square-mile town of approximately fifty thousand, the historic county seat. Students met weekly after school to gather water quality data for an ongoing study of a small source-to-sea river that had suffered degradation from channeling, agricultural and municipal well withdrawals, encroaching development, and high densities of nesting waterfowl. Students worked at streamside, taking samples and conducting physical, chemical, and biological tests at four locations on the river in fall and spring.

During winter, students built a database of their findings using the streamside locations as the "geocoded" points as links (or fields in the database) to existing GIS maps and database information from the town's GIS department. This was a partnership project funded by a state community service organization for capacity building between school and local government, NPOs, and local businesses. Well-developed GIS information at the town and county levels supported the student-generated data.

Two teachers in the science department, including one who had developed an instructional technology lab for student use, facilitated the project. Neither teacher had been trained in GIS use prior to the project, but both saw its value for environmental science. Both were Caucasian males. I have written about this project elsewhere (Alibrandi 1998). Students were responsible for presenting their findings, and they participated in a locally sponsored "River Day" event and in a statewide conference for environmental community service. The students were all Caucasian: four males and two females, and their grade level ranged from ninth and twelfth grades at the time.

School/Type	Community Type	Geographic Focus	Course or Project	Duration of GIS Use	Community Partner Type(s)
Baymouth: Local public high school	New England town	Local stream/watershed (17 mi, source-to-sea)	Environmental community service project	2 years	• Town government • Nonprofit land trust
Delany Middle: G/T magnet	Southeast capital county	State/satellites	GIS course/interdisciplinary project	2 years	• State EE coordinator • ESRI • Local GIS agent • University
Farr Tech: Magnet sci/tech HS	Major Midwestern city	Municipal planning/resource recovery	GIS course/project	Semester-long course; GIS in use 3–4 years	• Corporate sponsor • University • ESRI
DaVinci High: Magnet sci/tech HS	U.S. capital area	County/satellite data	Capstone course and project	4–5 years	• ESRI • USGS • NASA
Star School: Canadian private boys' high school	Major Canadian city	Municipal/provincial	Geographics course	3 years	• ESRI Canada • Statewide utility

Figure 3–3. *School Sites and Program Characteristics*

Delany Magnet Middle School (Chapter 5)

Delany is a "magnet" middle school for "academically gifted and artistically talented" students in a southeastern capital city. The school is located in a historically black community, and the students participating in the GIS electives came from the student body at large. At Delany, the initial teacher team was a combination of a science teacher and an instructional technology teacher who decided to collaborate on developing a GIS elective. One teacher had participated in a one-week inservice teacher-training course in GIS and water quality. The teachers were Caucasian females. Three other teachers, all females—a social studies teacher, a language arts teacher, and another science teacher—joined the project.

The students came from sixth to eighth grades, and those interviewed were one African American male, one African American female, one Caucasian male, one Caucasian female, and two males of Central Asian ethnicities. Most of the students interviewed had participated in more than one quarter of the elective course entitled "Satellites, Computers and Mapping" (Thompson and Hagevik 1999: <www.ncsu.edu/midlink/gis/courseoutline.htm>). The teachers involved had developed the GIS course as an elective, and found that students wanted to continue to develop GIS skills. The course has evolved with teacher and student interest into an ongoing offering. It should be noted that because the magnet school supports teachers to offer opportunities beyond the state-approved curriculum, avenues for innovation and experimentation exist there that teachers in other schools might never take.

Farr Tech (Chapter 6)

Farr Tech, another magnet school for science and technology, located in a major city in the Midwest, draws students from the greater metropolitan area. The teacher is a highly respected innovator and GIS technician, and has reached out to community business and educational partners. The (Caucasian male) teacher had instituted GIS in the context of his science courses, and had been teaching with GIS for three years. The students interviewed were three African American males, two African American females, and one Caucasian female. The interviews took place during a Saturday class; a partnership project in which a local business representative, eager to train and hire young technology-proficient workers, was involved in collaborative GIS instruction with the teacher.

It is important to note here that three of the five schools featured in the following chapters are magnet schools. The integration of this technology in classroom settings in the 1990s was far from a "plug and play" type of application. Since the pioneering work of the teacher featured in Farr Tech, the software for GIS has become more accessible, simpler to operate, and more ubiquitous in both government and commercial settings. The students in the Saturday class came from tenth through twelfth grades, and were interviewed during the weekly three-hour session they attended voluntarily. The entire course would extend over a sixteen-week semester, meeting every Saturday morning. Most of the Saturday students were students of color. I interviewed four African American males, one African American female, and one Caucasian female. One Farr Tech student's representation is presented in Figure 3–4.

Figure 3–4. *Representation of "Yourself in Your Community" from Farr Tech*

DaVinci High School for Science and Technology (Chapter 8)

DaVinci is one of the premier magnet high schools for science and technology in the nation. Located near the nation's capital, the county is home to the U.S. Geological Survey headquarters. If any school should pioneer GIS, DaVinci should, and has. Dana was one of the nation's first teachers to introduce GIS to the high school curriculum. She has been working to integrate the technology for five years. During that time, the software applications have undergone phenomenal change, and significant work has gone into developing more accessible software applications to attract teachers and school libraries to include GIS as an instructional technology.

Dana worked with a partner teacher, Hal, who conducts field studies in geology and hydrology. During my visit, which was year three for the teachers, Dana was feeling that this year had been the most successful. The course was a double-major "capstone" senior course designed to integrate science and technology in an original research problem. The community partner was a GIS specialist from the USGS who was interested in partnering to have students solve a real problem. Using satellite image data, the students were given somewhat random areas that corresponded to pixels of the satellite image of the county. Students visited and field checked the value assigned by the satellite imagery to the pixels that represented a square on the ground. This process is known as "ground truthing" the digital data.

I visited the school toward year's end, and students were scrambling to complete their components of an upcoming presentation at the county's impressive auditorium. Students were compiling data, refining reports, and constructing PowerPoint presentations. Dana and Hal allowed some of the students to be interviewed even in this extremely busy time. Three weeks later, I was able to return to see their presentations, where very knowledgeable audience members quizzed them on their procedures, and students reported that, among their other findings of over fifty USGS gauging stations throughout the county's river basins, only three had consistent data usable for their study. This the students reported in a county that houses many of the nation's elected officials. The students were confident, competent, and responded with assurance and candor to the questions. They were soundly applauded, and conversations ensued after the presentation much as in a professional scientific meeting or hearing. Some of the presenters were among those I interviewed.

The Star School (Chapter 9)

Innovative teachers Dan and Jack teach in a private boys' school in a major Canadian city. Pleased to be able to visit any school in Canada, where geography is taught in equal amounts to history, in the British tradition, I found the teachers utterly willing to experiment, to allow me full access to their classroom, and to carry on with their lessons, their in-class discipline, and their outrageous senses of humor throughout my three-day visit. The "boys," as all of the students are called, were dressed in varying degrees of uniform; green jackets and ties seemed to be the norm, but many "pushed the envelope" by forgoing the jackets, loosening collars and ties, or sporting bleached hair. The mood in the classroom was hectic and productive; there was an expectation of commitment to the tasks at hand, while strict codes of behavior seemed unnecessary.

I sat in a corner of the classroom, meeting with individual students who took time out from their teammates (they were working in pairs on specific problems) to complete the drawing tasks and questions involved in this study. It was a refreshingly offhanded and friendly atmosphere; not stuffy in the least, but the teachers were quick to point out that "just because it's a private school doesn't mean that each boy is a genius—kids are kids." To a man, each student described GIS as a tool for "problem solving." They weren't being coached to say this, but had apparently internalized the perspective. When I shared the students' comments about problem solving with their teachers, the teachers were pleased to hear that that sense had come through so strongly in the boys' own words.

Three of the boys interviewed were white and three were Asian American. Located in a proudly multicultural city with major Asian groups, Star's classes were diverse. Two of the Asian Americans were from subcontinental families and one was Japanese-American. The driveway and student parking lot at the day school are very active throughout the day, and while the campus is green and welcoming, the school, like most, is growing too fast for even its most recently built additions. Even the newest classrooms and laboratories were in full use throughout the day and after school. The GIS classroom was equipped with perhaps twenty computers, most of which were working. There was one printer and the room appeared as most computer classrooms do, but it was carpeted, so the noise level was somewhat dampened. Conversations carried on as students worked and teachers lent assistance, encouragement, cajolery, and authority as required.

The Schools in Summary

Teachers who collaborated on developing GIS options most often taught science, instructional technology, or geography. The geography team was a Canadian pair. In Canada, geography is taught as a major subject throughout the K–12 curriculum. In all of the U.S. schools, at least one teacher was a science teacher. In the one middle school, a more interdisciplinary project took hold, and data that was gathered in language arts classes became data for the GIS application. In the middle school studied, all but a math teacher participated in the interdisciplinary project. Interdisciplinary projects between history, science, language arts, and technology classes can be coordinated using a combination of GIS and other applications such as those for word processing, databases or spreadsheets, PowerPoint, or webpages.

Each teacher interviewed discussed the benefits of collaboration—perhaps the most important being the support needed during the steep learning curve of early engagement of GIS. Additional perspectives on application, data acquisition, and manipulation of the data were also shared in successful collaborations. As teachers and students learned more about how to use GIS technology, a synergistic effect of collaborative learning characterized the GIS classrooms. These teachers were not afraid to have students develop their own interests and inquiries. When those inquiries moved beyond the teachers' current capabilities, the teachers engaged community partners, other teachers, or technical assistants to guide their learning.

In each case, GIS use spread somewhat laterally across curricula and made new and more sophisticated projects possible. In the following five chapters, we get inside the schools that integrated GIS into various curricular applications. In each case, there was collaboration. In most cases, there was in-school collaboration and partnership with a community partner. In addition, in most cases, there was an actual field component as well as a virtual application. As we develop avenues for GIS use in classrooms, the integration of field and community work will greatly enhance the mutual benefits to schools and communities, and there is great potential for capacity building as a result of these collaborations.

Each of the schools had a partnership relationship with ESRI, developer of one of the most popular GIS software packages. ESRI has been the industry leader in supporting GIS in schools. ESRI, ESRI Canada, and now ESRI Germany and ESRI Australia have established personnel, Web support, and products directed at K–12 teachers and are the sources of support, research, and development in this new area of educational technology. By providing low-cost training and software to teachers, and by sponsoring the first GIS in Education conference in 2000, ESRI continues to lead the GIS-in-education initiative nationally and internationally.

Fitzpatrick had already worked with a national teacher network as a computer instructor with National Geographic Society (NGS)'s Summer Institutes between 1987 and 1993. NGS had invited cores of teachers from each state in the U.S. to participate, sending them back home to develop state geographic alliances to promote geographic education. From that sizable network of Charlie fans, a network of geographic educators became one of the target groups for GIS in education, but as you'll see from the following chapters, teachers with unique interests and backgrounds have come to integrate GIS.

4

The People Must Prove That There Is Water

An Environmental Community Service Project

The Baymouth case study describes an afterschool environmental community service project involving student volunteers from middle school, high school, community college, and the community at large. In the partnership project, a nonprofit land trust, a community college, public schools, and municipal agencies collaborated in water quality physical, chemical, and biological sampling and monitoring and mapping wetland and upland plants using GIS.

Benefits of Community Partnership

Funded by a state community-service organization through a local nonprofit land trust organization, this project bridged a major chasm between the schools and the town council. The land trust director served on the town council, which had been in fierce debate over school budget issues with the superintendent of schools. At one point, partnership meetings had to be held on neutral ground to avoid political risk. We will see how the project eventually led to a very positive impact on community relations. This in itself demonstrates the important juncture of GIS in school and community projects and partnership.

In the project, high school students mentored by community college interns sampled water from a local river weekly throughout the fall. Their four sampling sites spanned a twelve-mile stretch of the river, connecting additional upstream and downstream sampling efforts by adult citizen volunteers. The students located the exact points where the sampling was conducted using a Global Positioning System (GPS) unit under the guidance of a town GIS specialist (see Figure 4–1).

Figure 4–1. *GIS Agent, Student, and Town GPS Unit*

● The GIS Connection

Integrating GPS and building databases are the GIS Connections for this chapter (see GISC: "Building Databases for Integration with GIS" on the companion CD).

Ground Truth

The town had existing GIS maps and data tables into which the students' data were added as a field in the database. The town GIS map had embedded latitude and longitude locations, so the GPS coordinates could be located in the existing map even if the locations had no street address, which they didn't. Some corrections had to be made on the town map—by using the GPS, the actual locations of streamside sampling were used to ground truth the map.

This procedure is one in which data gathered from the field can be used to correct errors or generalizations found in a digital map. In this case, the location of the stream center (a line on the map) could be located more accurately. With accurate GPS readings—and the GPS unit was a high-quality unit owned by the town and lent to the project to complete its mapping task—the map could be ground truthed and redrawn with the new information. This is one of the important reciprocities that can occur in school/community partnerships involving GIS.

An additional understanding developed through this process is the realization that maps are not truth—they are representations, and this becomes very evident through the ground truthing process. We will see more examples of this across the school projects in upcoming chapters.

GIS data and information are exchanged readily in the U.S. between one political unit and another as a routine courtesy and policy. The town in this case used one type of software, the county another, but it was expected that they would share information. The partnership project required data from each entity and a third partner (a paid GIS specialist) requested that the two sets of data be integrated in one software. Since the two polities would

Figure 4–2. *Teacher and Students Entering Data at Streamside*

have to have done this at some point anyway, they worked through the technical issues to compose a map with both town-level parcel information and land use from tax maps and county-level environmental data.

Bringing in the Data

During the winter months, the students participated in computer applications training for ten weeks, constructing a database and incorporating the data into the GIS. From the data they had compiled, new analyses of the data were facilitated through spatial analysis with GIS. From a map representation, problem areas along the river could be isolated spatially. The results of their analysis led them to further refine their questions for spring fieldwork. Adding biological habitat assessments to their water sampling regime meant that they could refine questions about who or what was adding nitrogen into the river system. The data confirmed a suspicion held by the town's health department officer: that nesting birds were actually negatively affecting quality. The slow-moving pond was a popular "duck pond," where, near the road, parents and children would toss food to ducks, geese, and other opportunistic waterfowl. The resulting nitrogen buildup meant that a common practice was choking the waterway with increased nitrogen, feeding wetland plants that were proliferating and depleting oxygen and impeding water flow.

What had fueled interest in the river's health were the shellfish beds downstream that had been closed due to high nitrogen readings. Local residents who had traditionally gathered shellfish in the estuary were concerned because the clams, mussels, and oysters dug there had become unsafe for human consumption. Because shellfish are bottom feeders, they consume higher levels of nutrients that settle as sediment. The closing of favorite shellfishing locations has been a byproduct of increased development and population and their effects, and has become a chronic problem. As well, the anadromous herring that normally swim upstream to spawn in the freshwater lakes and ponds had been affected. Water levels were lower as results of withdrawals by residential and municipal wells, agricultural withdrawals, and golf courses.

Where's the Social Studies?

Only two laws protect the river: the Wetlands Protection Act, which limits any human activity within one hundred feet of the wetland, and the Endangered Species Act, which protects individual species in the river system habitat—the source wetlands, ponds, lakes, and tributary streams. The level of the groundwater table determines where surface waters appear. Cape Cod is considered a "sole source aquifer" in that its sole water supply comes from the groundwater; there isn't a feasible alternative supply that could be piped from elsewhere.

As state laws stand, it is only when a species becomes endangered, or if activities occur within one hundred feet of a wetland, that regulation or remediation will take place. In other words, the water in the stream itself is not protected by law, so if combined withdrawals completely removed all of the water from a stream, no one would be held at fault. Therefore, the onus falls upon the citizens to document the water levels in the streams, the numbers of anadromous fish observed in conjunction with those water levels in order to protect the stream, its relative health, and the species within it.

The students learned much more than water quality sampling from this project. From their hands-on actual experience and virtual GIS mapping of their findings, they placed first in an Envirothon competition based on land use issues. While water laws differ from state to state, the recognition of environmental law and its direct impact on public and environmental health will be essential social issues in the twenty-first century.

Community Service Learning

As part of their service to the community, the students presented their findings over a four-year period through "River Day" celebrations of the source-to-sea river. Presenting their sampling work, maps, and conclusions, they were a central part of the nonprofit land trust's gift to the community—a day on the river and its ponds with educational workshops, presentations, and recreation.

As contributors to the community, the students discovered an important link between a school/community project with families who came to enjoy the riverside event and learn about its ecosystem and its condition. In this way, their work of conducting social studies gave benefit to their research to the community, and, it was hoped, created a deep connection and responsibility to its sustainability.

Sustainable Benefits to School and Community

Even sampling the water can't change conditions overnight—the nitrogen loading had been going on for generations—but the students came to understand the complexities of the problem. Their data, when shared with the health officer, pinpointed a failed septic system that was addressed more quickly than ever would have occurred otherwise. Their very real connections with town office and agencies benefited both individual students and their school. At least two of the students were hired by the town for summer employment in the health department, coordinating more of its water sampling, shellfish information, and GIS information. The town GIS office, in upgrading its hardware, realized that the school could receive their used equipment because it was already municipally owned. So the school benefited by receiving equipment it might never have been able to justify in a school budget—a large format plotter.

The transformative effects of this project on the preexisting political climate of contention between the school and the town was more than timely, and points to some of the important mutual capacity building that can be facilitated through integrating GIS.

In Their Own Words

The activities described here took place in the context of a community service project; students were not required to participate, but came week after week to work in a natural setting on a small river. It wasn't glorious work; there were no fans or cheerleaders urging these adolescents on, but they described the project as "fun." The participating volunteers placed a higher value on environmental fieldwork than on the computer technology. GIS technology, in the participants' view, was secondary to the primary function of the actual environmental fieldwork. From their perspective, GIS technology was viewed as a tool for analysis and public education. In this way, the computer technology was seen to provide a virtual public education function within the context of their environmental community service.

Student Perspectives: How Did the Students View Their Work?

When asked to describe the types of technology used across the project, students lumped together the computer technologies (GPS and GIS) with pH meters, water testing kits, clipboards, nets, slide and overhead projectors, and VCRs. Student responses are shown in Figure 4–3. The responses are represented from left to right by chronological age; the youngest was an eighth-grade female, the oldest was an eleventh-grade female. The three middle columns are those of the male students in the ninth grade. While other students participated in the project over the course of four years, those in Figure 4–3 represent a core group. Much of this data is also described in an online *Meridian* journal article at <www.ncsu.edu/meridian/jun98/feat2-3/feat2-3.html>.

Perhaps due to their generational perspective, the students took a more wholistic view of computer use as just another tool. Chronologically, most of these students were from the "Class of 2000," ranging in birth years from 1980–1983. Students saw the use of GIS applications as *secondary* to what they considered their *primary* investigative learning; in this case, the hands-on (actual) water quality and biological assessments performed in the field.

The secondary students learned the GIS application more quickly and with less resistance than their college student and adult colleagues. Project par-

What types of technology did you use in your participation?				
GIS, GPS, water quality test kits, software	GIS, GPS, stream test kits, pH meters, flow meters	Water test kits, computers, flow meters, nets, clipboards, and field data–gathering equipment	Water quality test methods, pH meters, flow meters, GIS, GPS	GIS, GPS, slide projector, overhead projector, video, VCR

Figure 4–3. *"Technology" as described by the students*

ticipants from the community college, only a few years older, but not of the generation "growing up digital," demonstrated slower mastery of the computer applications. This tendency was even further marked in the adult participants.

Gender differences have been studied for decades (Liben 1995), but the introduction of a new technology in geographic education opens additional research terrain for investigations of gender and geography. About using GIS, an eighth-grade female student explained:

> It gave us a place to put our information and organize it. It helped us to actually see what we were doing in the field from a different perspective. It was easier to find the information after we put it into the GIS. (Alibrandi 1997)

Only the female respondents described this attribute of the GIS as a "place to put" information for its display. Figure 4–4 indicates possible gender differences in perspective on GIS utility.

Male students described the GIS and GPS as "connecting" their field data to the town's existing GIS land use maps. Thus, the sense of having provided real and useful data as part of their field study was enhanced by the computer application. Many volunteer water quality studies exist in isolation from one another and from other local data; it was through joining the databases using a GIS that the spatial analysis was facilitated. Without GIS, the data would have been hand-drawn onto a map to display the situated effects. With the GIS, successive years' worth of data can be analyzed and compared, both in spatial and/or in graphed formats.

In the final two comments in the chart below, two of the project's students had been hired by the town subsequent to their GIS training. Over the summer, they seeded shellfish beds, and using GPS, returned to enter their data into the town's database. It was nice summer work and another contribution toward a more sustainable community (see final comments in Figure 4–4).

	(female, gr. 8)	(male, gr. 9)	(male, gr. 9)	(male, gr. 9)	(female, gr. 11)
How did using the GPS benefit the project?	It told us actually where we were and gave us a place to put our information. It gave us a "downstream" perspective for measurement and comparison.	It hooked into the GIS and the data tables and maps and the program overall.	It helped us pinpoint the sites with true latitude and longitude, and to piece the maps together to connect the river with the GIS.	It helped us get a better sense of the maps and to pinpoint the sites on the map, and to connect to the interactive maps and tables in the GIS.	It made things more visual for us and for our presentations. It connected our data and made our case more professionally.
How was GIS used?	It gave us a place to put our information and organize it. It helped us to actually see what we were doing in the field from a different perspective. It was easier to find the information after we put it into the GIS.	It used the information from the GPS. The data we gathered, we entered into GIS to connect it with existing map information [layers].	To show "what our results were" to compare sites and comparative effects to determine cause and effects.	We used GIS to map the sites and to plot where high concentrations were nearby, and to analyze from the plot maps what the industrial uses were that might have impacts [or be point sources].	We were able to lay out maps and put all our information in one spot. It made it easier for us to look at all of our data and analyze it, to make it clearer in presentations and to review it ourselves.

Figure 4–4. *Student Perspectives on GIS Integration*

Do you expect that you will work with GIS in some future capacity?

(female, gr. 8)	(male, gr. 9)	(male, gr. 9)	(male, gr. 9)	(female, gr. 11)
I hope so! Probably in college depending on my choices.	We'll use it this year, I know that. It'll depend on whether I go into science or geography.	Probably—in marine biology or mapping the seafloor—in navigation or other marine science work.	Yes, I think it'll help me in the future—I used it this summer! I mapped the shellfish we planted this year. We also took the GPS out to the areas of high concentration and low densities [of shellfish] and coordinated them with aerial photos. We mapped some commercial and private shellfish grants. (These two students were hired by the town.)	Yes—I used it this summer! Probably doing fieldwork in college.

Figure 4–4. *continued*

In view of these students' comments on GIS application, a sequence of prerequisite skills emerged. Preparation for GIS instruction might include basic keyboarding skills, database and/or spreadsheet skills, basic geography, cartography, and orienteering skills. In this project, students constructed a database of their fall findings in computer lab sessions held during the winter months. One of the fields in the database was the x/y or longitude/latitude of each of the sampling sites. Data gathered at each site could then be located on the GIS map. The exact x/y coordinates were derived by using the town's GPS. The town GIS director had visited the project one afternoon to demonstrate the GPS and "gather the points" for accurate location.

Use of a GPS is an important community connection and data connection. When students gather data relative to an actual place on the planet and can then connect that place in the digital (virtual) map, the integration becomes part of their lived experience. The students gathered data over time, so they could begin to see in their data the seasonal fluctuations as distinct from "spike" events such as the failed residential septic system or rainstorms that might cause combined sewer overflows. Their understanding was literally grounded, but represented in the GIS. The GIS Connection (GISC) activity 4 illustrates how GPS can be integrated into a database for tracking events at a particular site over time. This is an important locus for conducting social studies.

Teacher Perspectives

The teachers have gone on to expand the project into the curriculum and have joined a regional group that is seeking answers to geopolitical watershed issues. About the benefits of the project, the teachers had the following comments.

- There have been lots of requests by social studies teachers for maps from the town—the teachers are learning about the technology and its products.
- Students are now our liaisons to the town and the town has gained the energy of its youth as active and productive citizens.
- This is a wonderful collaboration with the town. The town has shared its GPS/GIS resources, so we have expanded computer and GIS resources in the school.
- There is a new GIS course in the curriculum this year. Our work is spurring other courses to use GIS—in business courses and CAD courses.

- The new relationship of the open access computer lab has yielded greater visibility, funding, and utility by students and teachers.
- The project developed student leadership and career development— several of the students have been hired by the town already.

Since GIS is often municipally owned, it was viewed by parents and community members as an economically and environmentally beneficial use of technology for the community. Included among the community member comments below are those of the land trust director and the school's community service coordinator, local agents from the GIS department, the conservation department, and the coastal health resources office. Each had collaborated in the design and training of students and adult volunteers in the project.

Community Perspectives

- Through River Days, we've raised public awareness by presenting our information and communicating it using GIS. Before, we had arguments. Now we have hard data.
- When children are involved, and they're doing research in the community, there is greater consensus. The "trickle-up" theory really works! As a community member, whatever is done to raise students' consciousness raises the consciousness of adults also.
- The school has gained some tangible resources and a real-world multi-disciplinary project.
- The skills students are learning transcend the traditional boundaries of the school and have inspired new innovations.
- The community service is valued in multiple settings across the community.
- Through this project, the environmental organizations and agencies have made connections with the business community.

This last comment is important in building community cooperation that can aid in sustainability. Too often, the environmental and the business communities have been polarized. When the community's youth are involved, there is actually greater collaboration across previous community divides.

Parent Perspectives

- Students are a very valuable resource—they're full of energy, they want to work in the environment, and it's good economics. My son has shown me commitment to this program. School recruiters were most impressed by [his] participation in the . . . project.

- [The project] makes practical applications of skills students are learning in school, and enhances their interest and effort at school. Finally the concept of "slope" in math class had some practical application!
- The intergenerational aspect eases the transition from middle to high school to college level. Presenting at a university conference added significantly to [our daughter's] self-confidence. This experience has helped our daughter to make better decisions about her future.

Problems and Solutions Implementing GIS

At the time the project began (1996), ESRI had just introduced a mouse-driven version of their ArcView software. Since that time, ESRI's ArcVoyager product, included on the companion CD, and other user-friendly resources have been developed.

GIS training in an intergenerational group presented unique problems and implications. Middle and high school students were more "technology ready" than adults and learned GIS applications quickly. Adults progressed more slowly and became frustrated more easily. Out of this intergenerational training experience comes the recommendation that trained students become teaching assistants to aid adults and new learners in subsequent GIS training sessions.

The politics of school computer labs were at first daunting. Once a lab was scheduled, numerous setbacks such as viruses, electrical outages due to rain, and other factors conspired to inhibit the project. In an interim when the GIS instructor was taken ill, the teachers and project coordinators had students begin to build a database of their findings from the streamside testing. In this way, the data was "owned" by the students—they had generated, collected, and now entered it into database format so that it could be integrated with existing GIS layers owned by the town.

The student data was connected to a water sampling site location and through their GPS work, the exact x/y location became a field in the database that could be located in the digital map layer. The tables and graphing capabilities of the GIS could display differences from one site to the next, one date to the next, overall trends over the sampling period, and eventually annual and long-term comparisons. These findings were reported first to the town's health agent, and publicly at the River Day and state environmental conference (Snyder and Alibrandi 2002).

Lasting and Sustainable Benefits

An important enabling factor in this project was the central role of the land trust director, who was also a town council member. Her collaborations with town agencies had opened doors into the town for the school project. The benefits to the school related to this key player, and those benefits have continued to be important in ongoing school-and-community relations.

This project continued for four years, and participating students are now in colleges up and down the Eastern seaboard. Many of the students have continued with environmental studies and have reported to the project's lead teacher that their experiences have been very valuable to their subsequent studies and employment.

Additional benefits of the project—student training in GIS and its potential for teacher training or teaching assistantships—were unintended but successful outcomes at the school level. GIS and the continuing water quality monitoring project have subsequently become embedded in the school's curriculum. A new computer lab, accessible to all teachers and students, has been funded and runs ESRI ArcView software as a schoolwide resource. The computer teacher has instituted a system of student technical assistants, a feature we will see in many of the upcoming chapters.

In Summary

Many features of the Baymouth project will be seen in the upcoming school/community projects, particularly:

- ground truth
- community service learning
- students as teaching assistants
- building school-community capacity toward sustainability

As we proceed, my aim is that their applications will become more visible and possible as benefits of opening avenues of inquiry for conducting social studies.

5

Oral History, GIS, and the Web

Putting African American History on the Map

A Preface of Gratitude

The Delany history project grew from a relationship developed during a research project on school use of GIS. Out of common interests in GIS and an interest in conducting social studies for the community, the middle school and university faculty joined in partnership with a group of uniquely inspiring community partners. Cities in the Southeastern U.S. have unique stories that are the legacies of slavery and segregation. While parts of Delany's GIS project have been told many times, it has captured imagination because the medium of GIS was used to present and make visible that legacy in a new way, in a new technology, in a new representation, and from the comfort of the present looking back to the past.

The past is not always pleasant; it incurs pain on both sides of the racial divide that has been and remains an enigma to define. The "lines" at once infiltrate the most intimate areas of people's lives and the most mundane, practical, social, economic, and spiritual. I feel honored to have worked on this project, and am humbled and grateful for the experience. I learned far more than how to implement GIS in an interdisciplinary project, and because it would be difficult to separate my experience in this treatment, I will tell it from one insider's view.

All the while in my mind's eye there is a crystalline image of the power of this project, and that is the image of the circle of partners in our monthly meetings. It was a circle of students, teachers, professors, alumni, minority, majority, young, and old—a kind of reflection of the community at large . . . both Southern and Northern; those who had experienced segregation in their education, and those who had not. One had attended Delany when it was a segregated school, the premier black high school in the state; it was champion at sports and the center of black community leadership. There, at the center of that circle that has become an indelible image in my mind, was an energy that bound us to one another, to the project, to our future and how we could make it different, together. So while the story will move on to GIS and its role in the project, I ask you to hold that same image in your mind, because to me, that circle was near the center of how we create the future culture of community together in the simple way of talking and working with one another.

The Genesis of the Project

Curious to see how middle school teachers were integrating GIS, I began to visit Delany in 1998. The research I initiated there was the same project that led me to visit the other schools described in each of the case study chapters.

Delany is located in the traditionally African American quarter of the capital city of a Southeastern state. While it is now a middle school, it was built as a "separate but equal" high school as recently as 1953. While research and memory can tell of less-than-equal conditions, the school was a beacon of pride in the African American community. In the 1970s, the school was desegregated and converted into a magnet middle school. Like many in the U.S., the middle school has an eclectic architecture, with evidence of growth and additional wings expanded perhaps every five years. When I began to visit the school, there were several trailer classrooms perched in the small space between the main building and the housing project less than fifty feet away. The school buildings and trailers expanded to the full extent of its lot lines. A few grassy areas were marked off for science projects, with lettuce and tomato plants growing in checkerboard squares.

Delany enjoys a good reputation among the city's many middle school choices. Its reputation as a magnet school for the arts and academically gifted and talented students draws students now from every corner of the county school system. During desegregation, in order to meet the Civil Rights Act requirements, new school district map configurations had to be drawn. This expanded the city school system out to the full extent of the county. The effect was largely to disperse the African American students across the county schools, and reopen the formerly black high school as a magnet middle school to attract students to that part of the city. It worked, but as our teacher partners confided, there are still "tracks" within the magnet school— the neighborhood "base" population still is not fully integrated into the so-called academically gifted (AG) classes. In order to accomplish a balanced population, the GIS project teachers offered their courses as electives so that any student could enroll.

During the passing time between bells, the halls are filled with a cacophony of students of all shapes, colors, and sizes—the complete range of typical middle school adolescents. From three-foot sixth graders to fully developed females busting out all over, from tiny rails to massively over-weight waddlers to pushing-six-footers with the characteristic and fashion-able drooping drawers, the hallways are a picture of America's future population. All appear both utterly at home and equally uncomfortable with their physical, social, and sexual development, not quite in command of where their bodies begin and end. This is a unique time in adolescent development—in middle school, no teachers are lining up their students—they are expected to navigate the halls, attend class on time, and keep track of their assignments, gym clothes, and the ubiquitous book bags.

Once inside the classrooms, these unwieldy beings are led by wonderful and dedicated teachers who are innovative and willing to engage in all man-ner of inquiries with their students. There are three patched-together com-puter classrooms. Because of their status and some grant getting, the computers were robust enough to run ESRI's ArcView GIS program, Microsoft PowerPoint, Netscape, and several other applications.

The library, called the media center, truly is a center for the school. One day while I interviewed students there, a much larger university research project was being conducted there with some eighty students, and in another corner, the tetanus shots were also being administered! A typical middle school library day!

Two of the students I interviewed are from immigrant families from the Asian subcontinent, one girl is multiracial from the housing project, another is a white child of divorce, and one, an African American male, is a serious music student.

Directly across the street from the school, on the side opposite the housing project, is a row of characteristic "shotgun-style" houses—a some-what undersized bungalow design common to the African American parts of the South. Plywood is nailed across the windows of one particular house, and a sign reads "No Trespassing." In the surrounding neighborhood, at any time of day, young and middle-aged African American men can be seen walking around, not working, possibly dealing drugs. For the most part, they are not seen on or around school property, but they are within eyeshot of the middle schoolers.

A single tree that appears to have suffered extensive damage from the most recent hurricane has most of its root mass exposed and trodden bare by students and pedestrians. The schoolyard trees became an important rallying point for the school history project.

The School History Project

The project had several beginnings, depending upon where each of us was when he or she came toward it. Because it is a story of change, it could only be a story that starts in many places. One of those places was on school grounds, where the population boom and need for more space was causing two trees to be felled in the schoolyard. Two of the teachers rushed out to ask the destruction crew to save some slabs of the trees for posterity and the school's history.

The school's history was relatively obscured from its current middle school students, all of whom had been born after 1986. Social studies teachers must always place their students' lives in historical context; what do they know, what kinds of references would seem to be ancient history? The Civil Rights era was certainly "history" to these students, yet some continued to live in the neighborhood of the school. Directly next door to school property lay the parallel rows of townhouse-style apartments in the first housing project ever constructed in the capital city. This phenomenon was one that had bothered and intrigued me; this segregation in space and the resulting places it creates.

Another beginning was a rewarding project underway between the instructional technology teacher and some of her charges, who had been collaborating with an alumnus of the black high school. They had been developing a database of its graduates, class by class. The school had opened in 1953 and its alumni were (in 1999) moving toward retirement age when they could devote time to a project such as this. The alumni had remained very active with annual events and reunions, class trips, and cruises. Among the alumni were the capital-area sheriff, several legislators, PhDs who taught at the area's colleges and universities, both historically black colleges and universities (HBCUs) and the several other state and private institutions of higher education in the area. This team of the instructional technology teacher and the alumnus was a strong bond of commitment that set a tone for the project.

The instructional technology teacher had collaborated with a science teacher trained at a weeklong summer institute in GIS. After investigating the possibilities, they designed an elective entitled "Satellites, Computers, and Mapping" of which GIS would be a part. After two or three successful runs of the course, I had come to research the students, teachers, and community partners.

What happened after that research, the interviews from which I present in this chapter, was that some funding opportunities arose that could lead to our development of a unique project. It kept getting bigger and bigger with more participants until it included five teachers and their middle school students, three university professors and help from several others, college students, community GIS agents, state archivists, local librarians, dendrochronologists, wood products specialists, and of course, the alumni.

The project became ambitious, but amazingly, commitments to collaborate had a weight that carried the partnership project forward. Below is an excerpt from the planned activities as described in a funding proposal. The assistance of graduate students, one of whom was an alumnus of the formerly black Delany high school, was critical, particularly because many of the graduate students were students of color. Their investment in conducting the historical research was an important model for the budding middle school researchers.

What's GIS Got to Do with It?

This was a central question at one point when it seemed that the data was simply too difficult to connect in a GIS. At that point, the science teacher raised this critical question, "Why do we need GIS for this project?" as an acid test. As we worked through how we could represent the African American experience in a map, it became possible.

First, we would need a base map of the city with street-level information and a database behind it. GIS data comes as several layers and components packed together in a project. One set of information is in the database file with fields and records that can illustrate locations on a map. For example, using tax map information, the streets and parcels of land are visible. In the shapefile (.shp), the spatial representation is displayed. It might be an entire city limit, or a state or county. In this case, city-level street information was the best fit for the project.

But not all parts of the city housed or served African Americans, so less than the whole city was selected and depicted. This selection in itself causes a certain perspective to be seen. The representation of the African American community at all is a selection process that may never have otherwise occurred. All maps are socially constructed, just as are the interactions in every classroom. Educational anthropologist Frederick Erickson calls the moment-by-moment interactions in a classroom "micropolitical interactions" (1984, 525–546). In each of these interactions, teachers and students make choices about the ways they will interact.

Using Erickson's terminology, we could say that each of the choices made about the components of a map was a micropolitical selection. All of these micropolitical choices are made within a historical context, and in that context, either novel or traditional, innovative or mainstream choices can be made. In this case, the selection of a certain part of the capital that is rich in African

Month	Teachers (5)	Delany Students (125), grades 6–8	Graduate Students (6–12)	University Faculty (6)
November 1998	Begin expansion of GIS course	• Problem-based approach	Coordinate partners Archival and GIS research	• Assist in framing project questions and GIS
December 1998	List archival and GIS data needs	• Team problem investigations	" " Procure GIS data for classroom use	• Assist in historic buildings research
January 1999	Co-plan archive visit	• Developing oral history questions, techniques	" " Consult with teachers on pieces needed	• Assist in archival research • GIS technical assistance
February 1999	Conduct interviews of Delany alumni	• GIS mapping and Web authoring	" "	• Assist in linking Web presentations
March 1999	" " Transcribe audiotapes, edit videotapes	• Continuing research, mapping, and writing	" " Keep records, collect project data	• Review curricula, copresentations with teachers
April 1999	Prepare products: booklet, videotape, websites	" "	" " and survey students	Presentations: AERA, NCEE Product review
May 1999	Website preparation	Website preparation	" "	Copresent findings
June 1999	Final evaluation of projects		Report findings	Report on findings, administration, course design

Figure 5–1. *Project Time Line*

American history can help to change how it is viewed. If we give value to the area by mapping it, that value can go forward as a new community value. If the area is never mapped, its value is more difficult to literally make visible.

Conducting Social Studies

The social studies teacher and her students had an important role in identifying the historic landmarks in the community. Using two book resources, one in common with the graduate students—*Local Schools: Exploring Their History*, part of the *Nearby History* series (Butchart 1986)—strategies for locating, identifying, and researching significant historical buildings and landmarks in the community became the actual work of students. To see a complete list of the *Nearby History* series, visit <www.aaslh.org/publicat.htm>. This is conducting social studies. By identifying those locations, research at the state archives could uncover photos and street locations of the schools, churches, theatres, and shopping areas frequented by African American citizens. The eighth-grade social studies curriculum focused on state and U.S. history, so the project fit well within the "course of study" guidelines.

While some may focus on differences in the racially defined communities by highlighting signs of discrimination such as "Whites Only," only part of the story is told. African American life had a vibrance that was in certain ways diminished by the changes wrought during integration. The alumni spoke fondly of their community during the glory years of the pre- and Civil Rights–era. The school had been at the center of the community; it was a source of immense community pride. Once its status was diminished to an integrated junior high, its preeminence was no longer a gathering point for that community. But the alumni and the community do remember its greatness. Its glory was of another time, and the function and centrality of the school in the community have never been replaced by another institution. While churches remain a stronghold in African American communities, the symbol of liberation and emancipation through education as a unifying community agent is still lacking. (Two members of the project have written treatments about the significance of these schools in the pre- and Civil Rights–era South.)

Coordinating Oral History and GIS

In a model oral history interview, the journalism teacher videotaped a professor demonstrating interviewing techniques to middle school students in a journalism class. In the model interview, an alumnus spoke about different areas of the city, pointing out the classroom window toward them. Those references became references for the GIS map, the historical archival research, and the historical architecture class. The students were integrating oral history and GIS technology with the study of historical architecture and culture.

As one of the teachers put it,

> How often do social studies teachers get to teach social studies as a "lab course" in which students do research, interview people who made history, examine primary source material, then document that history? That's exactly what happened in this collaboration of [Delany] High School alumni, middle school teachers and students, university professors and graduate students, and community partners. This was not traditional social studies taught from a book. These students wrote the book and produced the websites. In the process, the middle school students and the adults learned history, geography, culture, and politics while they acquired skills in research, reading, writing, communication, science, and the use of technology resources.
>
> Though the [Delany] History Project emphasizes social studies, it gained depth and richness from its interdisciplinary components. Using a constructivist approach, students designed their investigations. The project evolved to reflect the interests of the students and the availability of resources. The students contributed a geographic information system (GIS) model showing a fresh interpretation of history. They documented historical information that might have otherwise been lost with the deaths of those who lived it. (Alibrandi et al. 2001)

Coordinating Historical Photos and Maps

Once these sites were identified, the search for historical background and archival photographs began. At one of the meetings, the teachers gave the graduate students lists of the archival pieces they needed to create a picture—a representation of visited and valued places. Another professor took the students on a historic city tour. She had authored a volume on the city's history, and gave the middle school students a look into the past in order to help them construct mental maps of the city in different periods of time. Writer William Least Heat Moon would call this process part of what is required to develop a "deep map" such as he described in his book *PrairyErth*.

Two of the stops on the tour were the GIS office and the state archive. Not many adolescents get an opportunity to visit an archive, but these students were shown early maps of the city. One that they saw was the collection of Sanborn Insurance maps, originally hand-drawn in the 1800s and successively updated with small pieces of paper pasted onto the surface—a layered map, but the older layers had become obscured by the more recent. After working with digital maps that could be updated easily, the students were struck by the crudeness of the old techniques. More assaulting to the adults were the very vivid map labels next to certain buildings on the map, such as "Baptist Church, Colored," "State Theatre, Negro," "Washington School, Negro."

On Sanborn Maps and Maps as Artifacts

The Sanborn Insurance maps were an immense national undertaking that developed in the early 1800s for the purpose of validating fire insurance claims. Drawn by hand in communities across the continent, each community's buildings were represented on the maps by their constituent materials. Buildings on the maps are indicated in yellow (wood frame), pink (brick), or blue-grey (stone or concrete block). In the days when entire blocks could burn, these maps were an important public information resource. They were generated in thousands of cities and towns across the U.S. and maintained for more than a century (see Figure 5–2). The Sanborn Insurance maps can be seen at the Library of Congress' website: <www.loc.gov/spcoll/215.html>. (For additional resources in researching Sanborn Insurance maps, see the resources section.)

While we're on the topic of historic maps, there has been some debate as to whether they can be considered artifacts. The late J. B. Harley, eminent map historian, maintained that indeed, historic maps are artifacts. As representations of the "known at that time," these maps were, of course, subject to those choices mentioned earlier. The size of a church or meetinghouse on a colonial map was often influenced by the belief system of the mapmaker. In Europe and Great Britain, there is a huge demand for maps of antiquity. As artifacts, curios, images of and into the past, they are the commodities of a brisk trade.

Harley (1990) maintained that maps were artifacts and that the choices of what was represented on the maps were also artifacts. Therefore the references on the Sanborn map, last updated in 1949, post-WWII but prior to the Civil Rights era, are representative *of that time*. Here is a parallel of what some mockingly call the "paradigm wars" between traditional ("dead white men's") history and "revisionist" history. Social studies teachers are now getting used to seeing the new perspectives in history that have become incorporated in textbooks, such as the inclusion of minority histories and immigrant histories as part of the mainstream. It's not that those parts of history weren't there, it's just that previously, they weren't represented. And the paradox is that if it isn't represented, it is, in effect, as if it isn't there.

Harley wrote about the need for geographers to recognize the artifactual quality of maps as social constructions. Thinking about all of those micropolitical selections as choices means that they were made within historical contexts and could either replicate the perspectives of the time or

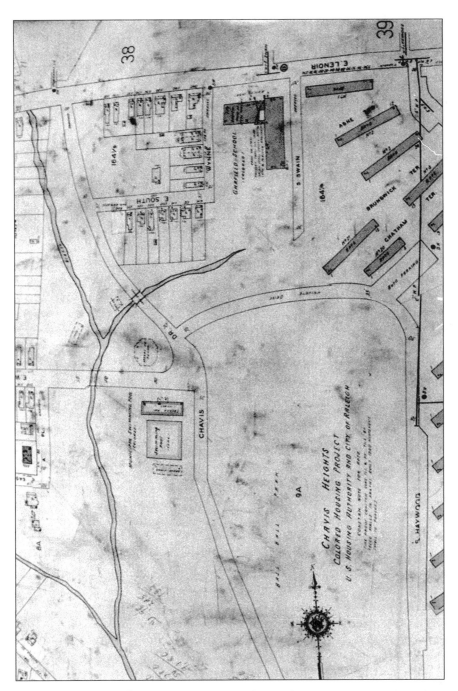

Figure 5–2. *Sanborn Map Image from North Carolina Archives*

innovate. The Sanborn map in question did not innovate; even through the apparent updates of insurance information, it was not updated after the Civil War to change the nomenclature or classification of buildings frequented by the freed African American citizens. Its representative choices reflected the social constructs of the Jim Crow period.

This issue of maps as socially constructed artifacts is critically important for teachers to understand if they intend to integrate GIS. Harley's colleagues have criticized GIS mappers who tend to think of their representations as "value-free truth." What they have demonstrated is that there is no one true map, although certainly satellite images and aerial photos are hard to deny. But any of the digital maps can be represented by certain interest groups, and the micropolitical selections made could total up to an entirely different map of the same place, depending on which interest group makes the selections. The political nature of maps can never be ignored. (To this end, I give assignments during military incursions for students to study maps presented in the media. Often, the images of the military hardware—the planes, the bombs, the targets—are grossly enlarged compared to the scale. These are the images on which the culture constructs its realities or beliefs about other places, "our" roles or impact in those places, and therefore our roles and identities of nationhood. Clearly, these are and will become artifacts, as have the war posters and maps from World Wars I and II.)

Visiting the City GIS Office

Another stop on the city tour was the city GIS office. Here, after viewing the Sanborn maps, students saw the digitally rendered map of the city's growth. As its population grew, so did the city limits. Highly contentious today because it determines who pays city taxes and who doesn't, the city limit is an ever-expanding sociopolitical construct. It is important for students to see the changes in political boundaries that have occurred within their lifetimes, lest they believe that "'twas ever thus." If they can see the expansion going on around them and understand its bounds in a political map, they may better understand the issues that will affect *their* paying taxes!

When students saw this GIS representation layered upon what they had seen at the state archives, new understandings of their city literally began to take shape. The city GIS director had an interest in history, but too often the city agencies are used by those interest groups that have a disdain for history, preferring instead to think of all places in terms of real estate value. The GIS director was pleased to speak with students about how to represent the past, present, and even the future using the new technological context of the digitized maps in GIS.

In Their Own Words

Teacher Perspectives

Their teacher said about their experience on the field trip:

> Several classes in the project explored the city's landmarks on . . . an important field trip for grasping the big picture. Starting at the city GIS office, the GIS director, a community partner, showed students an annexation map of the city. These digital maps displayed how [the city] had grown by annexation through time.
>
> Students and teachers were instantly able to visualize how the project could be organized and developed in a GIS model. She also provided annexation, street, and land parcel data for the project. Next the students visited the state archives, where an archivist displayed historic maps of the city in sequence. Students were fascinated by the development of the city and the mapping technology. 1923–1949 Sanborn Insurance maps vividly illustrated racial segregation, labeled with colored and white areas of the city. Students were startled by the reality presented. After viewing GIS maps of the city's growth, students toured the city and saw the features represented in the maps. They returned to school eager to communicate this historical information to others. With their new understanding and motivation, students persevered through the technical challenges required to create a variety of GIS representations.
>
> GIS students quickly realized that the data necessary to create historical maps had not been entered into official maps. They had to adjust digital information to show the locations and names of streets, landmarks, schools, and parks. The base layer for the project was a digital annexation map of the city. The original annexation data accurately portrayed the land as it was annexed, but some of the associated data was inaccurate. We corrected the data tables and conducted some ground truthing to assure accuracy. This required field checking and cross-referencing actual (ground) and virtual (digital map) features. The corrected data were returned to the city GIS office; thus, the project contributed a valuable public service to our collaborative partner and community.

Impact on the Student Learners

Armed with their new understandings of their city, of its history, of historic mapping, and with the new technology of GIS mapping, the teachers and students set out to construct a representation of their city in a particular point in time. The city GIS director contributed the data layer they could use as their base map. Then came the work of framing the African American experience on its own terms. The school community wasn't represented as a "corner" of the city, but as its own community. Some of the archival photos were timely, others weren't. Micropolitical selections had to be made—select those photos that best represented *that* era, and represent other important features in another way if there were no relevant photos.

The collaborative process sometimes bogged down in time lags. At a meeting, teachers would ask for a historic photo of such-and-such, then have to wait for a graduate student to get to the archive, search out the photo, order the copy, and review it, only to find it was a turn-of-the-century photo—not right. It could be frustrating. Any teacher who's ever advised the newspaper or the yearbook knows the territory! The amazing thing is, eventually a product comes out of the process! Indeed, the project was able to construct many products, but not without effort. This is the doing of history, the conducting of social studies.

In all, the journalism students videotaped and audiotaped twelve individual alumni. A graduate student transcribed the audiotapes and the middle school students wrote condensed versions, compiling them into a booklet distributed at the project year's culminating event. From the GIS elective and technology classes came the prototype GIS map and several webpages that told the story. See <www2.ncsu.edu/ncsu/cep/ligon/about/history/interviews.htm>.

Work on the alumni database continued with information that graduate students found. Individual students developed offshoot projects using GIS, such as a project investigating the impact of the railroad on the city's development and expansion. The historical architecture students did a presentation on prominent citizens of the African American community and prepared reports and a PowerPoint presentation on historic buildings and architectural styles in the community. A science teacher and her students had delved deeply into dendrochronology, designing a museum-quality exhibit for the school and using the preserved tree slabs as a backdrop for a time line of events in the school and community's history.

Most important, of course, was an exposition that brought together the alumni, teachers, students, and community members—the GIS director, parents, administrators, and even the Governor—to see how students could contribute to their community's history, and just as important, to its future, by understanding the past. (See <www2.ncsu.edu/ncsu/cep/ligon/about/history/esri/P7311.htm>.)

From a background in adolescent psychology, one professor praised the project for its incorporation of adolescents as "keepers of the history." When the adolescents were given adult roles of interviewers, authors, community historians, researchers, mapmakers, exhibit design consultants, Web technicians, they became contributing members of the community. This wasn't an exercise isolated in a classroom, or for viewing only by a teacher; these products were to become public information. This is the conducting of social studies for community.

Skills of conducting social studies. The skills that students developed were practiced and developed in context, for a purpose, rather than being discrete, formally tested skills. Think back to the haunting image by the student who depicts himself on a couch in front of a television and proclaims: "What community? I don't have a community." Clearly, that student had never been asked to interview a community member or to develop a product that would serve the community or help to engage him in his community. Teachers described the development of interpersonal, technology, research, and presentation skills as heretofore unequaled in their experience. Each felt that not only the students, but also they themselves had exceeded all of their expectations. Indeed, the collaborative project exceeded its proposed expectations, but its value to the community, especially through the various Internet-based products, is ongoing.

How much history did students learn? One of the critical questions to ask of such a project is whether students actually applied and transferred what they had learned to other areas—particularly U.S. history, but also the state curriculum, civics, and geography. In this particular system, those content areas wouldn't be tested until students went to high school and had matriculated in courses evaluated in end-of-course tests. From their visits to historic sites and the state archives, what did they learn about the keeping of history, of preservation and conservation? Follow-up studies of these particular students are being proposed to determine the long-term benefits of their participation.

Deep maps and spatial cognition. Some of the skills encompassed in spatial intelligence or cognition were described in Chapter 2. Consider whether students gained an understanding of the nature of change over time as expressed in demography and geography. The concept of multiple cultural perspectives on sociogeography is relatively complex, but these students had a firsthand role in developing products that represented those phenomena. Will their pattern recognition be aroused in viewing other issues using the understandings they gained from participating?

As students learned to identify architectural techniques and areas frequented by Civil Rights–era African American students, workers, shoppers, churchgoers, how did they incorporate this knowledge into their own understanding of the capital area? From their visits to historic sites and the GIS office, how did their mental maps of the city change? How were their actual and virtual experiences interpreted by them?

Community service learning (CSL). Most of the reflective part of students' learning was demonstrated in their presentations to community members who attended the final exposition, but because that event was held at year's end, reflective processing of their community learning—an essential component of CSL—may or may not have occurred. A reflection on this participation would be an important piece to include in a project of this kind, and would be an essential component in a follow-up study.

One of the school history participants has become a Web design consultant and has codesigned at least one educational website. Another participating student served as a teaching assistant in our university GIS in Education class, assisting adults with specifics of the technology. These students are currently still in high school, but their products have become valuable assets to the community.

Self in community. Building upon those developments, a look at the construction of self-in-the-community is an important component of conducting social studies. From a perspective based in cultural anthropology that has strongly influenced educational research in the past two decades, it would appear that the practice and value of adolescents' contributions toward sustainable communities are lacking in U.S. schools. Conducting social studies with GIS and other technologies is a way to reconnect adolescents to their communities in a contributory way. If we want to make the development of sustainable communities a goal of social studies education, we must include students as active participant-constructors of their community's social, environmental, and economic health.

Shared intellectual growth, development, and community. In addition, the idea that adolescents are sharing in developing an intellectual persona along with an intellectual community seems critically important when the educational community extols the social value of "excellence in schools." What does the excellence look like if not the development of an intellectual culture in which students develop their own contributions, feel valued, and are encouraged to commit themselves to sustainable democratic communities?

One of the problems is visualizing this new intellectual culture as shared and not exclusive to so-called honors classes or students. One of the closely held goals of the teachers involved in this project was the inclusion of students from all backgrounds. The courses were electives; they were not tracked. This is vitally important in an effort that aims to develop sustainable communities: all members of the community must be not only welcome but necessary. These are the underlying values of a democratic society—yes, decisions are based on majority, but participation is the most critical element.

Social studies as countersocialization. In so many ways, social studies education has become countersocialization because of the rampant impact of the media. So few children and parents recognize that making economic choices simply between products does not equal democratic decision making. In social studies, if we are to take our mission seriously, we must provide critical lenses through which students can see not just what is put before them, but what isn't and why not; what is considered history, by whom, and to what purpose? And why some history is presented and some not, or how to see what isn't told and see why not. As social studies teachers, we must be vigilant about the forces that shape what the society accepts as history, as geography, as economics, and so on. We must be able to turn the anthropological lens onto our own culture to see and understand it fully, lest we find again in another generation our students asking, not so innocently, "Why do they hate us?"

As humans become increasingly part of a global economy, we will see more political states changing. Will our students as adults be able to understand those patterns of change from their own experience? Or will they cling to a fossilized statehood and expect humans to continue to fulfill changing (increasing?) needs within the same old frameworks? This is antithetical to NCSS's themes of Culture and Time, Continuity and Change.

We must therefore recommit to present change as a constant, provide conceptual models for recognizing, understanding, and predicting change and give practice in the skills that can help students to recognize those patterns, be they political, geographic, economic, or sociocultural. As we who have logged in some history—both experientially and academically—can attest, the most important use of understanding history is understanding its patterns, not its particulars. If there are basic understandings of the motives behind historic events, then the sequencing of events can be predicted. Discrete facts only have meaning in context. When there is an experiential base, an ordering of discrete facts is facilitated. When students can identify the patterns of history, they can perform better on standardized tests.

Therefore, some of the skills necessary in using GIS become transferable skills. When students see behind the map to the database from which the mapped information is derived, a deeper understanding is constructed. Compare this process to that of simply viewing a paper map; there is no way to engage with the underlying database as there is in GIS.

Locating the ethical issues. As students use technologies, this same set of critical lenses must be turned upon the technology itself. How do the micropolitical selections involved in mapping exclude some elements of what is being represented? The parallels extend even beyond the scope of NCSS's Science,

Technology and Society across the multidiscipline of social studies. It helps to develop multiple perspectives that can be flexible, expandable, and non-static. This set of thinking skills is essential to social studies in order to learn to find balance among multiple perspectives, through research, revision, and review to incorporate new information with prior knowledge.

The ethics of the technology itself include such issues as public information vs. privacy, detecting competing values and users of GIS and GIS information, using GIS toward equity rather than for classist or racist purposes. Analyzing the inherent biases of a postindustrial society, its technologies and effects, we must also consider how and where those effects can lead to domination, subjugation, and cultural misunderstanding.

Conditions for Conducting Social Studies

Is there a place for conducting social studies in the curriculum anymore? How do we justify a skills-based interdisciplinary community history project in the face of high-stakes standardized testing?

In each of the schools visited, it was possible for teachers to develop electives. In Delany and DaVinci (Chapter 8), these were coordinated to be complementary courses. In the DaVinci model, the two were capstone courses that tied together a science with a technology; students selected among capstone combinations in their senior year. At Delany, the project spanned grade and academic levels because it was based in elective courses.

While these two schools are each magnet schools, their models could be made to work in any school. The question is, would administrators of schools fearing high-stakes test results be willing to risk a year of experimentation to see if original research would pay off? Obviously, educators in the magnet schools had made that choice. But why should this type of educational opportunity only be available to the fortunate few in magnet schools? Most educators would agree that at least one original research opportunity— a real research opportunity, not just a term paper—is absolutely critical to a successful social studies program.

I would recommend that in social studies, we take up the call to improve our students' learning, our communities, and our learning outcomes by introducing an interdisciplinary project year. Naturally, I see GIS as having an important role to play in an interdisciplinary project, and certainly that condition would be ideal for its integration. But neither do I promote that *only* interdisciplinary projects using GIS be called for, nor would I insist on the community being the focus. These would be negotiated among the teachers and students of each school. But I do think that that kind of structure and commitment on the part of a school for its students and its community are well suited to incorporate GIS and to enhance the learning and the community. Neither would I insist that in either middle or high school, the original research opportunity be held to a capstone position at the end of the student's matriculation. Quite the contrary. I think that a project of this kind would be an excellent introduction to a student's education, and an important transitional feature of a ninth-grade experience. In that way, the student's identity, his or her involvement with the community is more centered, includes the development of both an intellectual self and culture, and provides skills transferable across disciplines toward that elusive goal of excellence. In this model, I call for excellence of *experience* and as a goal for all learners, not an exclusive excellence, for it is ultimately it is the betterment of the entire community that is the goal.

Understanding History from a Grounding in Conducting Historical Research

When history can be grounded in material culture, oral history, and geography, there are multiple intelligences engaged. First, there is the inevitable linguistic intelligence, but as well, the kinesthetic and spatial intelligences brought to bear. Searching for, finding, and manipulating historic images or photos, or developing images of artifacts (such as gravestones, historic landscape features, or architecture) serve as a tactile connection to the past and to history. James Percoco in *A Passion for the Past* (1998) describes the importance of students engaging with these historic manifestations; statues, monuments, historic sites are all riveting, grounding community features that can help students reconstruct historic landscapes in their minds. These become layers in the mental map that can be used as flexible landscapes upon which history can be seen to have taken place.

In Chapter 2, I discussed the value of engaging spatial intelligence and thought as ways of storing information. The importance of mental imagery (mental maps) into which events can be "placed" or pictured as having happened is a fundamental strategy in reading comprehension. Using a GIS map to enhance any social study is a way to help make discrete factual information retention more concrete.

Time lines as graphic organizers help to depict sequences of events that can spur memory to connect additional information. In a GIS, this might be information that could be placed in a field of a database that could be projected into the map display. Again, entering the data into the database is a kinesthetic engagement with the data. While I do not equate working with actual artifacts to virtual data, there is a certain level of engagement that can assist in memory and retention—somewhat comparable (but to a lesser degree) to the difference between giving a map, chart, or diagram to a student vs. asking the student to draw the map, chart, or diagram.

Layered maps. Obviously the advanced practice of adding information into maps and creating separate maps that can be electronically generated is an important process for students to practice. While the maps are virtual representations, the processes students must use to construct them require analysis and higher-order thinking skills.

Of the NCSS' ten themes, possibly the only one not specifically addressed by the Delany project is IX, Global Connections. In fact, of course, making "Global Connections" was part of learning the basic GIS functions.

In addition, we've seen how many of the multiple intelligences can be brought to bear on those social studies themes and the skill competencies we believe important to learning in social studies. Left out of the mix are the interdisciplinary connections that help to strengthen the schemas or neural paths or networks that ultimately combine to become one's wholistic intelligence. That these pathways become active, flexible, and healthy are all part of a rationale for conducting social studies with GIS.

● The GIS Connection

The GIS Connection activities for this chapter include oral histories and GIS, photos and digital archives, and hotlinking photos to maps.

Where to Begin

The most useful reference for both graduate students and middle school students was the common text, *Local Schools: Exploring Their History* (Butchart 1986). In this book, part of the *Nearby History* series published by the American Antiquities Association, practical how-to guidelines for interviewing, finding archives and artifacts, getting permissions, audiotaping, videotaping, and preserving are all clearly presented.

Into the Community

If geography is everywhere, then anywhere in the community is a possible place to begin! If the school has a history, it's certainly the most convenient location for historical research. If not, nearby history probably isn't that far away—it's simply a matter of learning how to interpret or reinterpret the landscapes and their features.

"*Windshield assessment.*" This is a term used to describe preliminary investigations of a community. What are the nearby resources worthy of investigation? Are there derelict areas or features that could be researched, highlighted, and ultimately preserved? What a wonderful legacy that would be for students and the school to leave to its community.

Scavenger hunts. When I taught at the regional high school, I developed a map scavenger hunt in which teams of students had two weeks to gather resources to prove they had visited their town offices. This idea has been adapted to many uses. On the companion CD in the resources section, I include the hunt I devised as a model. Depending upon the political structures of your communities—be they towns, cities, counties—the specifics of the hunt would have to be adapted. But it's an important step in getting students to identify the various local government resources available to them, to get them acquainted with local government, and to gather resources that can be used in class.

Field trips and walking tours. When I taught a course called Teaching Geography at the University of Massachusetts, I included a field trip every day to get teachers to think about their communities as sources for geographic investigation. The town of Amherst, Massachusetts, had a wealth of historical architecture, a town common, and walking trails that identified both architectural styles and homes of famous authors and mapped the varieties of trees along the historic district. In an offshoot of the Delany history project, one teacher has continued with an ongoing environmental study using an ArcView extension called CityGreen, mapping with students the trees—both old and newly planted—in Delany's renovated schoolyard.

One useful publication entitled *Clues to American Architecture* (Klein and Fogle 1990) was a great tool for identification and discussion. I would augment this with two of David Macaulay's books, *City* (1983) and *Underground* (1983). The latter is particularly useful for developing three-dimensional understandings of places.

Visiting the GIS department. Whether your community is town, city, or county administered, there is most likely a GIS department nearby. These days, most tax maps (historically called cadastral maps) are being transferred into GIS formats. The GIS technician can tell you what kinds of information are available for your area and can usually provide low-cost maps for you and your class. In both the Delany and the Baymouth projects, local government partners were involved to help facilitate the sharing of maps and GIS data.

In Summary

Out of an initial half-year elective class, the Delany school history project grew across the middle school to five teachers, 125 middle school students, three professors, about a dozen graduate students, and several community partners, including the alumni. The project's products number over two dozen and include book chapters, articles, websites, the museum-quality exhibit, a landscape design feature on school grounds that has put the school on the city's Millennium Trail, GIS maps and projects, and a new awareness in the city that Delany is a positive and important part of the city's history.

6

Building Community and
Movin' On Up in Motor City

Farr Tech

Farr Tech is a premier magnet technology high school in a city known for its technological developments. On a Saturday morning, some twenty-five to thirty students are, like us, en route to a college computer lab. Driving in a van at 7:30 in the morning is Zach Z., who was one of the first teachers to pioneer the use of GIS in K–12. He unwinds the story of how he requested from ESRI's Charlie Fitzpatrick some of the original applications that have made GIS in K–12 more accessible. A unique and committed educator, Zach has spent much of his professional life in the public sector. Some of that time was spent with government agencies like the National Park Service, surveying federally owned forests and properties.

Zach is clearly a visionary thinker and educator. Farr Tech is the perfect sponsor of GIS in K–12 education. The school's mission is to educate students to lead the future of science and technology. The students in the Saturday morning class have no doubt heard about Zach, and they are involved in a partnership project to train high school students in GIS. The corporate partner is an engineering firm looking for recruits with GIS skills.

In Their Own Words

Teacher Perspectives

Says Zach of the Saturday course,

> It started January first and will go to the middle of May every Saturday. The Saturday after Good Friday we had off. There was another Saturday that they "gave" us off, but I told the students that I'd come in if they

wanted to come and seventeen of the twenty-seven were here, so they're very interested in the project.

Zach has collaborated on many such projects with other types of educational institutions. We will hear from a community college partner, a state college partner, and a nongovernmental organization partner as well as from a student. But first, it is important to hear some of the way Zach operates. He is an entrepreneur committed to education, using his networking skills to create partnerships that support GIS education across populations of students, teachers, professors, and community leaders.

As we meet some of Zach's partners, we will also hear about some of the educational issues inherent in GIS integration. What are the learning issues? The collaborative models? What have been some of the problems discovered along the way that can help others to design effective programs and projects? Many of the issues raised here will reappear in our final chapter on conclusions and implications.

Early Innovation

ZZ: I've been doing desktop GIS for about four or five years [this was in 1998]. When I discovered desktop mapping, the first time I saw it was at a teacher's convention. It just so happened that Charlie Fitzpatrick in ESRI's booth was next to the USGS booth at a conference. At that point I had some Toyota Foundation money for technology innovation and integration and when I saw what Charlie was doing with maps and data, there was no question—it was immediate that that was the thing that I needed to be doing for the kids that I taught in the city.

Making ESRI's ArcView Available

I pursued it vigorously. ESRI didn't even have a mechanism for how you would sell ArcView at the time! ArcView was the program used to view the maps you were generating in ArcInfo in a PC [since then, the mouse-driven ArcView has become the crossover software for ESRI's newest product introduced in 2001, ArcGIS]. So when I tried to buy the program, they didn't have a plan for how to sell it. I caused all kinds of problems for them! I actually paid them and purchased a copy of ArcView! It was a special licensed copy. I'm probably the only teacher in the world that actually has purchased a copy of ArcView! They should've refunded my money a long time ago!

After packaging ArcView for Zach, ESRI found that its popularity and utility flew off the charts. To certain user groups—particularly schools and libraries, and since then to others as a stimulus—ArcView software was given in kind as part of several teacher and librarian training programs. It is now available to schools at a reduced cost of around $500.

Because of my background in education and mapping and resource management for the National Park Service, landscape management and design jobs that I've done—well, gee, being able to map terrains and being able to put data and maps together—wow! That was just too spectacular! That made so much sense—it took the spreadsheet and made it a hundred times more powerful!

Early Work in Environmental History

ZZ: As a biologist and research scientist for the National Park Service, I worked on forest fire management studies in the late 60s–early 70s and actually spent a lot of time doing historic forest fire studies, documenting the role of forest fires and mapping out where we knew of a history. [In] the land office survey there's some very powerful information that can now be loaded into a GIS. Suddenly you can say, "Okay, now connect all of the places that have these certain characteristics—show me the contours."

That's pretty powerful when you can go back to historic information and look at present-day information and look at the changes! We have papers in *Forest Science*, a couple of papers in the Park Service archives, and in the *Smithsonian* on forest fire management. It was quite a controversy back then, the idea of letting forest fires burn. It was a radical idea then.

MA: But doesn't it do a lot of wonderful things for the regrowth?

ZZ: Yeah, in theory, but at that time, nobody wanted to test it out, until Yellowstone, when there was a revisitation to the concept. Yellowstone put in a million-dollar visitor center on the burn to reeducate people because so many people had the image that Yellowstone was totally destroyed. Of course it wasn't.

MA: So it was a quick jump to designing a course using GIS?

ZZ: Well, no! As I said, they didn't even have a mechanism to sell the stuff and of course there were no support materials with the software! Trying to find and obtain data—one of the data sets for our metropolitan area cost $4,200 dollars! And it provided you with street maps of seven cities and population data, but $4,200 to have information you could map in your own backyard—where was I going to find that kind of money? And of course, no one was even thinking, "What should kids be doing with this?" Charlie Fitzpatrick had just been hired by ESRI to get the Schools and Libraries program going. Today you have *Getting to Know ArcView* books that are wonderful tutorials. They have wonderful tutorials for the software. But GIS out of the box without any data and stuff was very user-unfriendly.

Students as Technical Assistants

I had to rely on a couple of students that were very interested in what I was trying to do. I could say, "Okay, I think we can do this, we want to try and figure this out," and they would go off and try and figure it out and come back and tell me their successes. So the kids had a little bit more time to think about how could you do that—sitting at the computer for any length of time—than I did for any particular class.

A year later, I wrote a grant for adult education in the public schools with the understanding that if the grant was funded, I would be provided a robust enough computer lab at Farr Tech, that I would teach adult education class in the evenings, but that I would have sole access to the spatial analysis lab [during the day].

[The Director] of the Central Business District Association [CBDA] began championing my work with GIS the day she heard about it. And Art Carter, the deputy superintendent of Governmental Relations who was in charge of adult education, championed what I was trying to do . . . and we got the lab.

So then, class-wise teaching became a reality. Also doing different kinds of things like kids doing PowerPoint presentations, taking their GIS work and dropping it into Word documents and learning something about desktop publishing and all of those kinds of things became possible. Internet connections and downloading different kinds of data and seeing how you could incorporate new data pieces into existing data sets became possible.

Connecting with Community

We did training programs for the [regional] Council of Governments [COG] during the school vacation. I had a three-day training activity— for twenty-four people who were going to actually be working with ArcView GIS tools in their capacities in the [regional] Council of Governments, and a separate half-day event for managers who might not be directly using GIS, but need to know how to direct their people. So we actually designed some customized classes for them right away. COG is only half a block away [from Farr Tech]. Then, having enough computers— 486 DX4 with 16 mg of RAM was fine . . . fifteen-inch monitors. At the time they were purchased, they were as good as you were getting.

Now with the latest versions of the software, I can't run ArcView 3.0 on a 486 DX4 with 16 mgs of RAM. We're in the process of doing a couple of different outreaches in order to fund the upgrade. The school doesn't have the funding. We don't have the administrative support you'd expect.

There are several people in the science and social studies departments at the school who have worked with us. The lab access is a problem right now—with only one room for ninety classes, there has to be more commitment for more computers for doing this kind of teaching.

Over the past four years, at least 150 students have had direct exposure to using GIS in problem solving. Others have used it as an additional piece for a project where students would come to me on an individual basis. Like in the advanced studies class we're going to, some of these students became introduced, and later decided to take the advanced studies class because they wanted to know how to use these mapping tools and I couldn't schedule just six or eight of them [for a whole class period in a computer lab].

Some of these students have created map products—one young lady had a very nice display—she downloaded data layers from the Centers for Disease Control on health statistics and then mapped that information looking at the relationships between population demographics and health considerations. Through the EPA's 307 Toxic Superfund site, she looked to see if there were more of those sites in lower-income areas and also whether there were more health problems in those areas.

The GIS Connection

The activity relates to the above student's map—the idea of site selection for an agency or a business is a classic spatial problem. The whole "business locators" industry now incorporates GIS into its analysis for clients looking for a location. See GISCs on site selection: "Where do we locate the next daycare center?" for a site selection activity. This kind of activity is a great way to get students to use some of the functions of ArcVoyager.

Community Service

> Right now I'm trying to finalize [collaboration] with Gleaners. They're a food bank operation and they've asked me to help them understand how the agencies that get food from them could better service the needs of the hungry, so we've mapped some of that information. Now they're interested in having some of the students come in and work with them. AmeriTech has approached Gleaners about giving them some money because what they want to fund is some technology education initia-

tive. So I'm trying to help Gleaners imagine that we could have high school students working as the "technology mentors" with neighborhood food delivery agencies like Gleaners. It would be easy for us to set up a lab at Farr Tech and invite the agencies to come in and work with students. Because Farr Tech has students from across this whole area, we could invite students that lived within particular areas of the agencies, and they would become the agency link. An agency representative and a high school student that would work with that agency would train together. AmeriTech would supply money for the hardware and Internet connectivity and we'd have this training center so that we could do all kinds of additional spatial data training activities.

From the Central Business District Association, I was receiving a newsletter in my school mailbox once a month. So I read in the CBDA newsletter that they were doing an inventory of all the abandoned and vacant buildings in the CBDA, and since the CBDA was across the street, I made a call, and spoke to the president. I introduced myself and said I'd read about what they were trying to do with this inventory, and said I think I have some tools that I could share with you. She set up business meetings to come to Farr Tech. We developed a complete multilayered GIS for the CBDA over a couple of years. I worked with the engineering department at [a] state university. So that was a very positive situation that led to meetings and associations with several business leaders all over the community. And nobody really knew about GIS, so [the CBDA director] became a champion of it on our behalf.

The head of the civil engineering program worked on some of the CBDA project—a graduate student was developing the inventory and I did the GIS for it. So I talked to the university about putting the software and computer lab over here, but they couldn't afford it. But we have a public school program for gifted and talented students. So our public school license for the software could be extended to [this community college] lab if we were using it for a public school program, so we ended up increasing everyone's capacity that way.

School/Community Capacity Building

At this point in Zach's commentary, we entered the classroom where some twenty-five students were arranging themselves in teams at computer stations. I interviewed six of the Saturday students during the class. We sat off in a corner and students drew their representations and answered my questions, talking with me about their college plans, their lives, and their interests in GIS, among other things. I found this response particularly telling—the student's image of himself in the community included a computer (see Figure 6–1). He describes how he has integrated his new GIS skill set and tool in his understanding of himself in his community.

Student Perspectives

S: Of course, I'm in the middle and I'm surrounded by all the things that are important to me on a daily basis. There are a lot more things that surround me, but these are the main things. This is music—I love music; not just rap music but music in general. This is our school, geometry and chemistry are *not* my favorite subjects, but this is an example of schoolwork. Um, this represents church, basically. I'm a Christian, so . . . That other part is computers, I deal with them every day. This in the corner is about helping people, 'cause I believe in that a lot, cause it's good to help in a way. And the rest is GIS that helps other people get information that they normally wouldn't be able to get on their own. And family and friends of course. My family is very important, my girlfriend, my mom, basically.

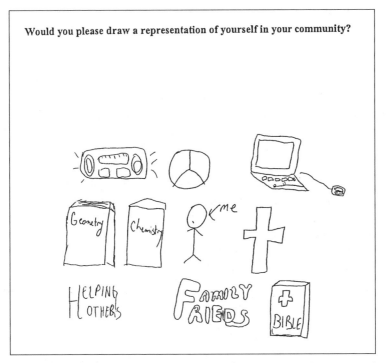

Figure 6–1. *Student Representation of "Yourself in Your Community" from Farr Tech* Compare this representation to the one depicted on page 53 to see how the Farr Tech student integrates self, community, and GIS.

One of the most unique gifts Zach brings is an understanding of institutional capacity and how to maximize it for mutual parties. Whether it's the state, community or technical college, an evening adult education program, a local business or business organization, or a government agency, Zach has contacted his potential community partners and has developed collaborative projects with them. These projects come back with mutual benefits to the school and its community partners.

In Their Own Words

Let's hear from the community college partner and find out how the collaboration evolved.

Community Partner Perspectives: Vera

Vera: I had taken Zach's GIS for adult education class, just to get more familiar. We knew each other years ago when we taught at a private middle school. When I did the original [grant] proposal, I called Charlie Fitzpatrick, who told me, "By the way, there's someone in your area that's doing some interesting things with GIS." So I went over to talk with him and realized, "Hey, I know this man!" Small world!

I'm the PI [grant's principal investigator] and wrote the original concept paper and brought the various partners together. I was looking at a way to increase the enrollment in my GIS class at the community college, and trying to develop a way that my students could transfer to a four-year program more readily. A very large proportion of my students work. And I thought, "These kids are not making enough money to pay their tuition and take care of themselves." And I thought that this would provide them an opportunity to develop some skills that would give them a decent paying job down the road, to help pay for their education.

Some interesting things are happening with two of our counties. They've both entered into multimillion dollar contracts with ESRI. Both of these county entities will need large numbers of people trained in GIS, so there's growth in that area. It's estimated that there's a need for thousands of GIS trainees.

MA: What's the politics of GIS in this state? Is GIS analysis for taxation cut along county lines, city or town lines, or is it state-generated?

GIS in the Community

Vera: Individual planning departments—some of them in this state are using paper maps, some are using CAD programs, some of them are using

GIS, but they may not be using ESRI products. It's a hodgepodge at this point. Two counties have taken the lead and are the top two counties in population and wealth, and I would think that there will be a push toward standardization.

One of those partners describes how Zach brought together a project that is reaching out to four high schools to work with teacher teams to integrate GIS. Nan is an environmental teacher educator working in a multi-school GIS teacher/student training project.

Community Partner Perspectives: Nan

Nan: Zach's a very sharing, partnership type of person, so he contacted various people and that's how I found out about it. He got in touch with [the state college] and I think we were all at the national conference and Zach pulled all of us together and we were talking about this and that's how it started.

With this partner who was part of the instructional team for the high school outreach project, I discussed some of the mutual benefits to schools I'd worked with. She agreed and had seen many of the same results, particularly those relating to the cotraining of students and teachers in GIS. She describes some of the additional benefits to the teachers involved in the GIS integration project.

NS: That's almost one of the key features of th[ese] program[s]—that they are a way for these teachers to get online access, and better computers. The teachers we're working with on this program are getting priority over other teachers to get this technology up and running because they're willing to put in their time on this project. And GIS, I think, is really helping to push that in a lot of these schools. It's not only for GIS, but it's for teachers to get email and Internet access, so I think it's important in that way also.

MA: What are your impressions of secondary students using GIS?

NS: I don't think they'll have any problem! We had students at the workshop I did for the pilot project. Each teacher brought one or two students with them. What we did for the workshop is, we had a student and a teacher working together and the reason we did is so that the students could help the teachers with the technology.

Actually, at one point—it was a two-day workshop—the two students were getting impatient with the two teachers! And so they convinced the teachers to let them work together for awhile, and the teachers let them do that, but then the teachers found that they [themselves] were falling so far behind in the class that they had to drag [the students] back.

But, what happens with the students is that they whip through the exercise because they don't really care about what it means, they just want to click through it and get it done! Then they immediately start getting on the Internet and messing around!

Because the students are so far ahead, they can pick it up so quickly, they almost don't even need the training. The training is really for the teachers to become comfortable enough to let their students use it. But it's the teacher who designs what the students are going to do in the class.

Students as Teaching Assistants

NS: This one teacher had taken an interesting approach because he didn't feel real comfortable with computers and so, for his watershed project as well as for the GIS, his plan was to let his students learn how to use the software, and to use the students to train the next set of students. So he didn't feel that he had to know how to do this as long as he could get his students to train the next ones, and his students were really up for that! They had no problem doing that. So that was one way of approaching the technology issue!

Listening to Nan describe the plan this teacher had for integrating GIS through student technical assistants intrigued me. Currently, I am working on a model in that vein. The potential for integration through direct student training toward technical assistantship seems promising. Among the avenues toward GIS integration, it may be significant if indeed students are to become the active participants.

Community Partner Perspectives

Training in the technology was often shared across partners in the teacher-training project. One of the partners, from a state college, originally comes from China and brings an incredible skill base to the partnership.

Yuan: I've done a lot with GIS customization, system development integration of GIS with urban modeling, environmental modeling. I did a lot of projects with EPA. And funded by EPA and [a regional] commission, we are doing a lot of integration of GIS and the Internet to coordinate basinwide data (six states).

My background is in physical geography from China. I came here in 1998 as a visiting scientist sponsored by World Bank and got a master's degree in the U.S. in urban planning in the U.S., but my PhD is in

GIS and urban modeling. When I came here four years ago, [we] had no GIS, so I tried to get funding through grant writing or through projects, so I worked with the Kellogg Foundation initially to do some watershed projects, so that's how I started. Then I worked with the Army Corps of Engineers, and as part of that project there was a mandate on public education for elected officials—what they call a technical briefing. So frequently I give presentations or even one- or two-day trainings for EPA offices, Army Corps offices, and so on. So this is how I began doing outreach and training. So that's the main reason I began to move toward GIS in education.

We have a mission here [at the state college], and I graduated from the normal university, the teaching university in China. After I came here, I moved to technology activity and research and now I'm back to where I started. I love teaching!

I've worked with Zach on several things. We have two proposals and keep in close communication. He was able to do some very sophisticated training with high school students. I had heard a lot about him, and I appreciated what he was doing, so I contacted him.

I enjoy working with them—the three of us enjoy working together [the community college partner, Zach, and Yuan]. Every department here has a preservice teacher program, so when we went forward with an NSF proposal, I suggested we add this preservice component for future teachers. So those five or six pages actually won the grant for us!

Yuan's background as a GIS technical partner is broad, deep, and essential to ongoing support for teachers involved in the collaborative project. These partners have continued to collaborate on subsequent grant-funded projects to involve teachers in GIS integration since my visit in 1999.

In Summary

We've now seen a variety of educational programs and initiatives integrating GIS. From Zach and his associates, an understanding of the centrality of the services GIS can facilitate, the various partnering opportunities, and a bit of history help to round out the continuing story. Zach's partner described some of the dynamics of students and teachers learning GIS and learning how to incorporate it together, co-constructively.

Zach himself states that he relied upon his students to move forward in the technology and discover its functions, to teach him about it. He sees this as simply an efficient and effective distribution of responsibilities. This mindset is one that I believe reflects a sort of map of the new landscapes of learning. In most of the high school settings discussed in this book, we see how teachers in both the U.S. and Canada have adopted this mindset in order to integrate GIS technology.

Zach moves so fast through projects and initiatives, it's kind of hard to keep up with him, but some of the key points he's raised and demonstrated have been

- GIS as a community resource and tool
- Capacity building through school/community partnerships
- Students as teaching assistants
- Students as community technical assistants and employees

Preview: Interlude

In the next chapter, we pause and reflect upon some of the issues and social phenomena that surround GIS integration. In each of the three preceding chapters, we've seen fundamentally different educational dynamics at work. We've seen how teachers, community partners, and students relate in collaborative ways to conduct their studies. These and issues relating to the Science, Technology, and Society theme are raised in the "Interlude," and a social studies classroom in inner-city L.A. is highlighted.

7

Interlude for a Critical Perspective

Are We Bridging the Digital Divide?

Now that we've heard various perspectives from those who are and have been integrating GIS in a variety of ways, let's examine some of the critical issues I believe necessary to keep in mind while considering GIS integration. Beyond the pitfalls of hardware, software, funding, retraining, school schedules, and administrative and community support, there are larger issues that should be brought to bear on discussions of GIS integration. As if those weren't enough!

Many of the teachers interviewed commented on their students' backgrounds. From three inner-city schools where racial diversity was evident in the GIS student population, to the major city private day school where diversity was evident but economic class was a major factor, to the capital area's science and technology magnet and the New England public high school where diversity was more of a problem, we must all address the "digital divide."

Many of the students I interviewed had computers at home and had used them for quite some time. Their familiarity with computers probably led them to participate successfully in a course or project of this kind. Others came to the courses or projects to develop computer competency. But as we've heard, GIS isn't a "plug and play" application. It is best encountered after some degree of familiarity with other software applications. At Jordan High School, Herschel Sarnoff's students themselves have mapped the data on computer ownership, access, and other socioeconomic issues.

One concern I have is that GIS not become available only to certain students. Because it is used in so many fields of industry and agency, the skills are such that they should also be distributed evenly. For North Carolina

teacher licensure, a required technology portfolio must demonstrate competency across several computer applications. GIS would satisfy many of those,
but more important is the social value attached to the requirement. By
requiring that all new teachers be technology-proficient, the state is placing a
value on technology integration into the classroom as a means of leveling the
playing field for students. As we look at technology integration, teachers'
decisions have significant social implications. If we as teachers do not integrate technology in the relatively equitable landscapes of our classrooms,
then the social reproduction of class and race will remain unaddressed.

There are enough inequities built into the educational system already
that must be overcome—tracking, separating "gifted" from "base" students
in magnet schools, inequitable recruiting for prestigious courses and programs, school redistricting, and even pure demographic distribution. I have
concerns that the ubiquitous GIS technology remains untaught when the
skills could mean gainful employment and upward mobility. Certainly we
saw Farr Tech students using their Saturday class as a means of addressing
these goals via expanded career pathways. In this chapter, we'll see GIS
taught from social studies teacher Herschel Sarnoff's perspective. In his
classes, the issues of Science, Technology, and Society are addressed head on.
In the section "In Their Own Words," Sarnoff shares what he calls his "hidden agenda" of career development for his students.

"The Color of Water" and Critical Perspectives on Technology

"The Color of Water" refers to the title of a book by James McBride, who discusses the complexities of growing up in a multiethnic, multiracial family. To
her African American son, his Jewish mother responds "the color of water"
to his question, "What color is God?" (For more on *The Color of Water: A
Black Man's Tribute to His White Mother*, see.) The issue here is one of *data* and how it is gathered,
generated, analyzed, and represented. In the next chapter, I refer to this as
understanding the processes *behind* the data.

Between the 1990 and the 2000 U.S. Census, immense changes in race
and ethnicity took place. A major problem for the Census Bureau in 2000
was how to address those changes using a format that could be statistically
compared to the previous decades' format. Would they change the race and
ethnicity classifications? Would they increase them? In the end, the Bureau
used the same classifications they had used in 1990, but suggested that
respondents could check more than one box or classification, whereas in the
past, they had been asked to check only one.

What would this mean for census data and its relative "accuracy"? For one thing, there would be respondents for the first time who claimed multiple ethnicities. Will these be compared as an aggregate? Will individual reports be identified so that a comparison of one's self-identity in 1990 and in 2000 will be compared? How will the new data affect programs directed at specific racial or ethnic groups? Some organizations were suggesting that their members fill in only one classification so as not to "water down" the statistical advantage of its constituent minority.

An important consideration is what USGS partner Jay identifies as skepticism (see Chapter 8). One's skepticism should always be brought to bear upon map products, because as discussed in Chapter 2, those products are representations; the representations are based on perspectives, biases, and beliefs that guide how the mapmaker will select, generalize, include, omit, and otherwise represent or misrepresent *data*. Mark Monmonier has written several books with such titles as *How to Lie with Maps* (1990), and he doesn't mean reclining!

The Difference Between What *Is* and What Is *Given*

Data—from the Latin verb *dare*, to give (singular *datum*)—means literally "those that are given." Data must always be understood as simply *part* of the whole, not the essence. As with other media, consumers are too willing to accept the information represented in a map without questioning the origins of the information, the selections made in the presentation, or the inherent biases of those producing the map.

The most articulate critic of the social implications of GIS has been John Pickles, whose book *Ground Truth: Social Implications of GIS* is an important antidote to blind acceptance of GIS data, maps, and policies derived therefrom. Says Pickles:

> GIS itself has a poorly developed archive and virtually no critical history of its own production.(1)
>
> . . . because of the high cost of its development and use, GIS [is] a tool and product that changes the way certain groups and organizations operate . . . As such, it is an important element in changing social relations in market economies; in producing new demands, commodities, and forms of domination in the workplace; in developing new systems of counting and recording populations; in defining, delimiting, and mapping space and nature; and in providing new tools and techniques for waging war. (1995, 4)

It was one of the chapters in Pickles' book that guided the Delany history project. The chapter addressed the inequities inherent in a national mapping system in South Africa under apartheid. Who owns the technology, what information they gather and consider important enough *to* gather, and the way in which the information is gathered, aggregated, and represented are all elements affected by a biased sociopolitical environment.

While the phrase "we have the technology" is often used in jest, it isn't just the "we" that is potentially dangerous. These concerns are part of what the NCSS theme of Science, Technology, and Society would have all social studies teachers address. But the fact remains that there are invisible biases and lenses that are difficult for us to detect.

Of all of the students I interviewed, only one articulated this issue, and that is because of the painstaking processes the teachers and students encountered as they tried to deal with data. The data that were given were blithely claimed to be "85 percent accurate." Yet the DaVinci project partners in Chapter 8 saw an opportunity both for the federal agency and for their students to examine and challenge that assumption more closely.

As many of the postindustrial nations transition toward "information economies," we can ill afford to consider all information as anything but data—"those that are given"—and not truth per se. Even as the U.S. Department of Defense perfects their satellite-guided weapons and GPS-guided personnel efforts, we must recall the social implications of not being represented and the determination of the disenfranchised to use our own technologies against us.

Maintaining an ethic of equity in spatial representation and problem solving will be one of the most important concerns we face in the coming century. ESRI CEO Jack Dangermond promotes "GIS for everyone" and has begun training foreign geographers in an in-house master's program. A heavy dose of ethics and equitable democratic principles may or may not be part of that curriculum. I therefore see a responsibility for U.S. social studies teachers to understand and eventually master this technology, not just to the point of making "nice maps" but for investigating legitimate social, historical, anthropological, sociological, economic, environmental, and ethical issues as integral to social studies inquiry. I also recommend *Beyond Maps* (O'Looney 2000), which addresses choices and decisions made by the GIS administrator for local government. O'Looney presents examples from several communities in the U.S. that illustrate GIS use by parties with competing agendas.

Further, the reason that GIS must be taught in a context of critical and ethical perspectives and practices is that it could possibly be abused. Bear in mind Pickles' caution that this is a weapon of war. GIS-guided weapons are in use as I write these words. Knowledge of utility lines, tax parcels, and other publicly available information could be considered targets for students bent on destruction. Therefore, the integration of students' contributions *for community* is absolutely critical in conjunction with GIS teaching and learning.

Community as Energy

> The twentieth century concludes in much the same way as it began—with the redrawing of maps. However, the new maps are not so much of geographic territory, but of landscapes depicting new and developing networks of finance, people, and culture . . . The ultimate work of education is to learn to be a human being . . . But as we struggle for new identities we must be able to transcend these notions of territory and engage new concepts of energy and place. (Hartoonian 1996, 6–8)

In many ways, the twenty-first century begins as the twentieth century did in North America: with great influxes of immigrants adding texture and vitality to its communities. At the same time, it is an opportunity to reconnect with the values of the continent's ancestral cultures. In the interim, certain understandings that unite ecology and culture; those values of diversity, both biodiversity and cultural diversity; and sustainability, the ultimate measure of human existence on the planet, constitute a new base for communities under social reconstruction.

Learning Based in Community

One of the most important lessons I learned from fifteen years of classroom teaching was the importance of the school-community relationship. But not just for the community; it was most important for the students. Hartoonian's words about "energy and place" vividly echo my experience in teaching high school freshmen. I taught in a regional technical school in a geographically isolated region, Cape Cod. It might seem to the outsider that "Cape Codders" would have a strong sense of region and place, and that had been my adult experience. But the Cape Cod of an adolescent's experience is still relatively provincial. By freshman year in high school, many students had never been "over the bridge"—in other words, across the Cape Cod Canal to Boston or Providence, let alone New York City or Washington, D.C. In the longitudinal study I described in Chapter 2, conducted with six high school students, increasingly complex understandings of geographic space was demonstrated over the four high school years during which these adolescents became licensed to drive.

In the 1970s our social studies department recognized that students lacked preparation and understanding in geography. By 1978, we had instituted geography as the ninth grade introductory social studies curriculum. Somewhat later, in the mid-1980s, when national studies on "geographic illiteracy" raised awareness about the problem, the integration of geography and the need for teacher reeducation in geography led to a massive project by collaborating national geographic societies and organizations to address the need (GENIP 1987).

During that fifteen-year period, the Cape was defining itself as an ecological region with unique water resources and problems needing attention and protection. We followed the case now known as the infamous one featured in *A Civil Action* (Harr 1995), which was local news for us throughout the 1970s and 80s. Taking place less than fifty miles away, the horrifying story of Ann Anderson, the polluted Woburn, Massachusetts, neighborhood wells, and the deaths of eight leukemic children regularly appeared in regional news media.

It was in this context of regional self-definition that our learning and my teaching of ninth graders was situated. Therefore, the community and the classroom were utterly dialogic, as in our class we investigated the emerging debates and growing pains of a peninsula with fragile groundwater resources beneath all of our twentieth-century activities. We studied the issues and held student elections on regional referendum questions. I would happily run into my students attending town meetings and public forums, but the voices of students *in* the discussion were virtually absent, save our announcements of student voting results to local radio.

In the classroom, I was beginning to see my work in teaching as "energy management." Working with the dynamic of student energy can be understood at a palpable level. Managing the energy of young people to help them learn how to manage their own energy is a major part of what teachers do. There are many ways to manage the energy, but if the teacher sees her job as preparing students for living both independently and collaboratively, she must provide opportunities for student practice in responsibility taking and decision making. Therefore, it is critical to channel energy in a dynamic way in which students can recognize their own mastery of self-discipline, attention, and learning, but more important, their own *contribution*. Minus this, students simply replay and pattern themselves after narrow roles as consumers.

Our classroom and community were situated within in a broader culture characterized by competitive forces, so I often felt that my work as a teacher was countersocialization. In a postindustrial cultural setting where prolific media compete for consumers' attention, generating "wants" that fuel an economy based on constantly developing goods and services, a focus on *learning* can appear naive, misguided, frivolous, or even heretic. As the textbook (three billion dollars a year) and testing (five billion dollars a year) industries increasingly dictate classroom activities, a focus on learning appears ever more irrelevant.

Youthful Energy, the Missing Function in Postindustrial Communities

The cohesion of a community is often expressed as the strength of its networks; individuals are tied to others through social networks of shared experiences, resources, and commitments; networks are experiential, physical, familial, and economic. From an economic standpoint, if a community is a unit of natural, human, and capital resources, that community would be unwise to squander any of its energy potential. And if the energy of a community's human resource is left underutilized, that energy will find ways to manifest itself. In the case of the young members of a community, there is mounting evidence that that energy can either be directed into prosocial or antisocial behavior. We label electrical energy as positively, negatively, or neutrally charged. It is time to see students' energy and to channel it.

In other than postindustrial societies, youthful energy has a *function* in the community. In agricultural communities, youthful members have pastoral or horticultural responsibilities; their roles are essential to feeding the community. Traditional societies may be more efficient at directing and respecting youthful energy as essential to the community, simply because those communities cannot afford to waste their energy. But in postindustrial societies, a great waste of youthful energy is being exploited by various industries. Youth are prey to the media, while dealers supply recreational vehicles, drugs, tobacco, alcohol, junk and fast food, and other youth market goods and services. The insidiousness of tobacco industry advertising campaigns directed at addicting youth was recently revealed.

The economic *function* of youthful energy in the U.S. has become that of *consumption*. What is the eventual result of this one-dimensional cultural initiation into adulthood? How is it that parents feel they are providing for their children by buying them ATVs, video games, designer clothing? Youth market advertising (another multi-billion-dollar industry) impels consumers—both children and parents—to substitute real interaction, guidance, and upbringing (which are difficult) with extravagant purchases intended to demonstrate endearment, status, prestige, beauty, or machismo.

If young people are only able to participate socially through consumption, they will see and construct their roles and functions in the community in the same vein. The fragile and critical juncture of adolescence, rife with identity crises, is a time when active participation should instead be focused toward the community as a whole, with the adolescent an integral part. While U.S. crime has decreased, the youth share of crime has increased. The disturbing recurrence of adolescent violence aimed at schools should ring a deeply resounding message. Are we listening?

School as Holding Tank

Rather than support a contributory community function of students, schools have in fact replaced that function with a "holding pattern," in which students are expected to perform within narrow roles, but not *functional* roles in the community. Youths' roles are seen as "extracurricular," having the function of entertaining the community as students participate in sports, arts, and competitions.

There are exceptions, such as vocational/technical schools, where secondary students' work actually does have a community function. Through technical schools, community members are served by students. In auto mechanics, childcare, culinary arts, cosmetology, graphic arts, health occupations, horticulture, and other vocational occupations, students provide services to and interact daily with community members of all ages. Vocational/technical schools are not segregated in an age-grade environment devoid of elder and younger community members. But so-called academic schools are places where the "real world" ends. While some attempt to integrate real-world problems and authentic assessments into the curriculum, there is no sense that these must in any way have a functional relationship to the community.

The Forbidden Curriculum

By forbidden curriculum I mean the erosion of teachers' curriculum decision making as supplanted by standards, frameworks, textbooks, and the imposition of standardized tests. While a modicum of any of these constituents in an educational experience might be reasonable, the combined impact of national, state, and industrial interests in the curriculum render community-based learning and teaching nonstandard, irrelevant, and unsanctioned. In the forbidden curriculum, certain secrets should never be discussed, because the content of the curriculum has been designed by some higher authority.

One of the secrets, of course, is that to understand the interests and forces that shape the economy, the institutions, and the society means that one would see oneself (as either teacher or student) as a pawn in an economic system that rewards mastery of content held in certain (purchased) textbooks and as measured by certain (purchased) tests. To think critically against this social construct is rendered irrelevant, so that particular discourse is forbidden.

Recall Akhlaque Haque's cautions about GIS that remind us that the tool may either be used to dominate or to empower. At the same time, some decision makers relegate certain neighborhoods inner city, slating them for urban renewal. The values of the dominant consumer culture (malls and chains) outweigh community values (historic, ecosystemic, socioeconomic). Developing an understanding and teaching both with and against this dynamic was the forbidden curriculum taught at both Delany and Farr Tech.

Another big secret is knowing how to critically assess those industries; how to determine whether they utilize sustainable practices; whether they actually contribute to or destroy the planet's resource base, and if they don't positively affect the planet, how to redesign them so that they do. One of the secrets that got out during the past century is the concept of the "green corporation" or corporations moving toward social and environmental responsibility. These remain the exceptions, but why are they not studied as models for the future? The "new" fields of social history, minority history, women's history, and environmental history are still, after thirty years, trying to gain entry into mainstream curriculum, even while they have permeated mainstream culture. Who's holding the cards?

The ultimate secret is how to decide what an individual can do, and why an individual would choose to put his or her human energy toward one particular goal or another. This decision is to teach as if living consciously were the norm; therefore it appears quite out of touch with a consumer-based reality in which choice making and decision making revolve around consumer choices. Let's acknowledge that adolescents' spatial and social search skills are being distracted, captivated, and exploited by producers of consumer goods such as computer games, CDs and videos, ATVs, skimobiles, and other teen toys. Why are these skills not utilized in schools or for the community?

Is the forbidden curriculum really forbidden? Effectively, yes, because all but teachers of students in private schools (not subject to standards) must focus on preparing students for standardized tests. These tests in some cases will determine not only "how well the school is doing" but, as in North Carolina, can be used to punish some systems and reward others monetarily. While some teachers who have addressed the gaps in both their students and their communities do develop responsive curricula, others are impelled by the mounting forces of market-driven education. Thus, to understand how one's own mind works, to know how to trust it to judge, weigh options, measure resources and consequences, and, thus informed, to act, are becoming luxuries apparently only the elite can afford—those same elites who will continue to run the legitimate corporations.

How We All Lose

When youthful energy is lost to the community, there are a number of effects. First, the future of the community is not nurtured because there is neither investment nor inheritance. Second, youth lose a sense of being *part of the community*, and seek (but do they find?) acceptance and identity from their peers and their consumption of products. Third, generations are lost who would have developed interests and skills, and learned the values of keeping the community sustainable. Instead, youth increasingly become alienated from it, yet dependent upon it, but without a sense of being part of it or having an investment in it.

Schools should rightly see themselves as central to the community, and there is no doubt that they are one of the most cohesive factors in a community precisely because of the youthful energy within them. Sadly, the institution of the school, rather than serving the central function as the location of community cohesion, has become increasingly disconnected from the real world. While theorists argue about the canon to be taught in history classes from textbooks printed elsewhere, the idea of social studies has become a hollow term; almost no one actually conducts any social studies in secondary schools. It is no wonder that young people become alienated and communities disintegrate. The disintegration of family units, neighborhood, community, and sense of place characterizes postindustrial society.

If chaos and complexity theories are applied, the disintegration need not continue indefinitely. Indeed, archeologically and chronologically we have seen communities, primarily due to their viable geographic locations along rivers, crumble and be rebuilt throughout prehistory and history. *Rather than removing youth from the community, the question is, can we redefine the institutional function of schools to revitalize communities by directing youthful energy toward sustainability?*

I make a distinction here from the "student as worker" model offered by Sizer (1992). Although the "student as worker" is similar in suggesting that students' work has value and is respected, its context still remains within a traditional curriculum and has little relationship to the community. What I am suggesting is to expand upon the model of the technical school that serves the community by seeing schools as *functional* in the community, not limited by the narrow definition of just educating a community's youth. It is time to recognize that schools are central *to* communities, where students contribute *to* the community, are recognized *for* that contribution, and find their places as necessary and respected members *of* the community.

Provided with prosocial, contributory options, young people can fulfill needs and functions that are valued and respected in the community. In the current political and educational turn-of-the-century frame of reference, the prosocial manifestation of youthful energy is known as "community service." While community service is valued, it is an extracurricular activity or at best, a "subject." But there is a fundamental difference in missions that state that a school will "develop in students, x, y, and z" from those that state that a school will "develop *students* as *contributing community members through* x, y, and z." The energy going into the school is not coming back to the community in the ways that it could.

We believe that an important element in redesigning the function of schools should include the application of GIS. One long-term school project utilizing GIS has gathered enough data in an Ohio watershed to have become a major player in its community. Through GIS, the school and its students are providing multiple services to their community: water quality monitoring, rare species reintegration, and GIS analysis.

Consciously Bridging the Divide in Watts

Certainly, the possibilities presented in the previous and following chapters illustrate how GIS can facilitate this process. In the next section, I introduce Herschel Sarnoff, a social studies teacher from the Watts area of Los Angeles. He is a thirty-year veteran of the Los Angeles Unified School District (LAUSD). Herschel and his students are demonstrating the critical and ethical uses of GIS in social studies.

In Their Own Words

Sarnoff, a teacher in LAUSD's Watts region, has been teaching GIS since 1999. Consciously bridging the digital divide, Sarnoff selected to work in an inner-city setting, training in the 1970s. He finds that urban schools can offer a certain freedom of instruction and opportunities for funding for projects.

Teacher Perspectives

Says Herschel,

> I love the kids I teach—they need good teachers, too. I taught history with computer-based activities and I used to run a social studies computer lab for the school. I've been integrating technology for twenty-nine years, but when I saw GIS, I could see its potential. It took me fifteen minutes to see how I could apply it and the waves parted! Poor schools can get technology—I have my own server and LAN. I think I'm teaching the way most people will teach in twenty years.

Partnering with Teaching to Change L.A. (TCLA) gave the GIS class a new emphasis. The inequities of resources and other issues came into focus. "TCLA helps teachers in the inner city. They got excited when they saw what we were doing with GIS." TCLA had data on uncredentialed teachers and other educational issues. Sarnoff and his students developed new themes from the tabular data and could relate it to existing data such as educational attainment, income levels, and other census data. This blossomed into some

fifteen to twenty projects, many of which are posted on the Web at
<www.tcla.gseis.ucla.edu/divide/teachers/lausd_jordan.html>.

The GIS Connection

For this chapter's GIS Connection, we recommend you visit Herschel and
Jordan High's GIS websites to see the types of GIS projects students are conducting on the conditions of their lives and on spatial and demographic conditions that shaped historical events.

Herschel's projects and reflections are "MUST READS!"

Reflections on Students' Learning

> This sharing of knowledge makes them kind of sparkle—their thinking
> goes to another level, and they show other students how they do the GIS. I
> make them do an analysis—*Why* the North won the Civil War—from
> looking at the information. There are two ways of teaching with GIS—
> canned tutorials on the website or from the book vs. a project that hasn't
> been done yet, so we're going up a level by doing a project.

Another indicator for Herschel is that

> They come in all the time—other than when they have to be there for
> class—they run in at lunch. In the morning, they come and get passes to
> come in later in the day—they're really proud of their Web products.
>
> The kids get recognition and they're part of something. I tell them that
> this is college-level work. I see how kids are responding to this—you're
> enjoying teaching when you see how the kids respond!
>
> Definitely it's a higher level of thinking skills. The connection between
> data and the spatial representation hits all of the learning modalities—
> visual, textual, kinetic. When I had the social studies computer lab, I used
> to teach everybody's students. I've only had five or six kids who couldn't do
> [GIS] in the four years—out of five hundred.

On Co-Construction with Students

> We have meetings—we're peers working together—using collaborative
> learning and teaching with the kids—we're equal partners in decision
> making on the project and we decide together what we're going to do. We
> construct the data dictionary. The teacher is the team leader, but for exam-
> ple, a student may pipe up and say, "Mr. Sarnoff, Pedro knows how to do
> that!" So Pedro demonstrates the procedure. My first year, I had some
> really bright kids and they pulled me though. I had my GIS students come

to my U.S. history class to work with the students in the history class—they can teach each other better than I can, so it was great.

On Sustainability and Uptake of GIS in School

Herschel has been teaching GIS since 1998, but understands that the continuation of GIS classes is tenuous. Trying to address the "lateral uptake" issues of GIS sustainability in his school, he says,

> I want someone in my department to pick this up—I'll be retiring in three years and this is a gift we're giving to students—when you think of all the skills involved in using ArcView, it's immense! Right now I'm teaching teachers for four hours on Saturdays. They're from several high schools in LAUSD from all different disciplines. I'll teach other teachers how to make maps for their classrooms, how to integrate PowerPoint. My students help them—kids are fighting to be the teaching assistants in the Saturday class!

Among the many insights and observations Herschel shares on his various websites, he notes the following, from <www.tcla.gseis.ucla.edu/divide/teachers/lausd_jordan.html>:

- The existence of GIS is unknown among the vast majority of teachers, and a way must be found to spread the word.
- Teachers who use GIS are scattered, and some method should be found to bring them together. Teachers are poorly paid and cannot be expected to fund their own attendances at conventions.
- ESRI and other GIS companies are beginning to recognize they must get more involved if they want more K–12 students exposed to GIS.
- Some funding mechanism must be found to allow creative teachers the time to write GIS lessons. Classroom teachers work all day with no opportunity for research during their school day.
- Corporate, university, and governmental GIS users should seek out and support teachers using GIS in their classrooms.
- GIS has the potential to become a major player in the tools available to educators to motivate and develop technology skills for their students.
- School boards and school administrators need to be informed about the uses of GIS in the classroom.
- As a teacher of twenty-eight years I have never seen students so involved with learning. I have never worked as hard as I have with my GIS class and have never enjoyed teaching as much.

Coming Up

In the next chapter, we move to some in-depth interviews with community partners, teachers, and students who engaged in a capstone course—a full-year investigation of their community, integrating field work and GIS. In offering these examples, I ask all social studies educators to consider deeply our commitment to developing in students a sense of what Barbara Winston called the past-present-future focus. Certainly Herschel and the teachers we've heard from so far and those we'll meet in Chapters 8 and 9 are committed to teaching in a past-present-future-oriented landscape of learning.

8

Getting Behind the Map

Critical Thinking and Community Service Learning in the Capital Area

DaVinci High School for Science and Technology is debatably the most advanced public high school for science and technology in the U.S. As such, it should have been and was one of the first in the nation to integrate GIS. Located in the same county as James Percoco's school, there are admittedly significant community partnership opportunities available. This raised expectations on the quality of the project. But there are opportunities for community collaboration using GIS virtually everywhere in the U.S. and Canada.

DaVinci's county is one of the fastest growing in the nation. Since the 1970s, its population has doubled and its once rolling green hills are now almost completely overrun by town houses, condominiums, and strip malls. What had been a rural landscape has been utterly transformed by burgeoning development. This gave rise to a massive increase in impervious surfaces—in other words, asphalt and rooftops had replaced surface areas once cloaked literally in green pastures, forested areas, and normal soils.

We'll visit with two teachers, a significant community partner, and two students to get a view inside this unique school and program. DaVinci's program features particularly good conceptualization for conducting social and environmental studies through GIS integration for interested schools.

A Capstone Course

The unique feature is a capstone geosystems course that had evolved over a four-year period. The capstone concept is a yearlong culminating senior experience that integrated science and technology in an authentic research project. This was a double-credit course with both fieldwork and a computer lab. Another unique factor of the concept of the capstone course was teacher collaboration, where the technology served the field data the students collected for their geology class.

GIS Community Partnership

In the capital area, the community partner worked at the U.S. Geological Survey. A pioneering GIS educator, Dana had always been active in seeking partnerships with government agencies—they were nearby, and, as federal agencies, committed to sharing information and to public education. This is a particularly significant feature of integrating GIS—sharing information is part of the culture of the technology—at least in the U.S., where information generated with public funds is considered public property (we'll see a different dynamic when we go to Canada).

In Their Own Words

In JJ, Dana found a fabulous community partner—he came with experience in teaching as well as with the technology, and had the foresight to ask students to do actual fieldwork along with the virtual software and digital data. This section comes from an extensive interview with JJ, recorded in his federal office.

Community Partner Perspectives

JJ: I started with GIS before it was really called GIS. Digital Cartography. That was undergraduate, and then I went to graduate school . . .

MA: Where was the undergraduate work?

JJ: University of Connecticut, and then University of Nebraska at Lincoln for my master's degree in geography, border resources. That's actually where I started teaching GIS. I taught a master's course in GIS, and then taught undergraduate classes there in math and aerial photo interpretation. [I] went to work there at the Center for Advanced Land Management Information Technologies or CALMIT, which is a consortium out in the Midwest for advanced remote sensing and GIS technology. I started teaching GIS workshops and remote sensing workshops to local government and soil scientists and university faculty. From there I went to private industry to a company that produced a geographic information system. They're out of Canada actually. I was an application specialist with them, which meant that I helped users of the software apply GIS to their problems. And in the process of doing that, did a lot of training in GIS worldwide, actually. In some cases to teachers, but mostly to environmental professionals and nonprofits and clients of international aid organizations.

One of the clients in that process was the U.S. Geological Survey and I did a lot of work in the GIS research lab, which was the USGS facility for spreading the use of GIS throughout the bureau and actually throughout federal government. I was a demonstration training specialist, so, I did a lot of applications work, but my primary goal was to demonstrate the utility of GIS to VIPs and other folks and to train people in the use of GIS. So as part of that I started training teachers at DaVinci High School, and started taking interns and volunteers from "DV" to do project work in the GIS lab.

MA: Oh, wow, so high school kids were volunteer interns?

JJ: Uh-hmm. Or paid interns in some cases.

Then I started a geographic information system for a local watershed. I was actually doing research. I think that's probably when I started working most closely with Dana, when she came to that workshop, and started talking with Dana about having her students work there. That was in 1993. So that was the start of her partnership. But all along I was sort of helping her with the GIS and then when it came time for our county to build their geoscience curriculum, where they want to have GIS and remote sensing within the curriculum, Dana and Hal and some other folks from DaVinci came out to the survey and met with myself and some other folks.

Community Service Learning: Student Internships/Community Liaison

A critical component in this partnership was the student "mentee," whose internship with JJ was an important communications link between the class and the community partner. As an alternative to the capstone course, seniors could elect to be mentored. The role of the mentee, who became a liaison between USGS and the geosystems course, is an important model to consider.

JJ: They started talking with us about the geoscience program, and I'd been talking with Dana about that, and then the most recent activity came about as a result of a mentor-mentorship program at DaVinci. A ment[ee] came out here, and frankly, I kept saying to him, "What do you want to do?"

MA: This was a kid?

JJ: Yeah, he had worked a lot with hyperspectral imagery and remote sensing, and I kept saying, "I want you to pick a project and do something you'd enjoy." And I think it just came down to he'd enjoy . . . anything. So Dana came in and said, "Well, we've really been struggling with a project for the class to use. *What if we use this mentor activity as sort of a gateway?*" And so she said, "What sort of projects can you recommend for our class?" And that's where we came up with accuracy assessments and the impervious area study, which is something that I've been trying to find time to do for a long time, and haven't been able to.

I've had a lot of applications experience with GIS. I've used it in a lot of different fields, a lot of different disciplines, and what I loved about the job I had with GIS Research Lab is that I was working with people from hydrology, geology, air quality—all these different environmental and health applications. In fact, that's what I've done through all my jobs.

I think that's one of the toughest parts for teachers, is having a good idea of what to use GIS for! And that's part of what's real important, I think, in the partnership, is having somebody who has a good idea—what is it you're going to use GIS for? What's the scope of the problem? What are the important variables? What data sets have to be done right, and what ones don't necessarily have to be? I mean, those are all the sorts of things that . . . someone who's using GIS professionally has a feel for that the teachers don't yet have experience with.

CALMIT had a very good applied bent to the work, and a lot of students came whose technical skills were phenomenal—as they are at DaVinci. We had folks coming from out of the country who were sixteen years old and working on a master's or PhD because of their math skills and computer skills, but had no idea what you use these skills for. So they were there to get a feel for, "Ah, here's an erosion problem. This is what an erosion problem is." And "these are the variables we need to measure." And they could write two thousand lines of code in a GIS package to get it done, but they didn't know what it was.

That seems to be a really common . . . missing link for a lot of folks, even GIS educators at the university level—they talk about data structures, and talk about the formalisms of GIS, but what do you really use it for? How do you use it properly is a much different story.

Here, JJ is addressing the gap between GIS application and education. In this case, the technology is clearly ahead of the educational system partnership. The interdisciplinary nature of a GIS that combines databases of varying types of information extends beyond traditional disciplinary boundaries. JJ continues:

JJ: I think probably my influence is through DaVinci itself. Because the way they're implementing this is through a pilot structure. So they have five pilot schools, and DaVinci is the lead pilot. Providing them with the questions to answer is probably the greatest role that I've played in the whole process. Because again, we communicate quite regularly and I'll go out to the school. The students will have come up with different ways of approaching the problem, and like it or not, my job is to sit there and say, "No, that's the wrong way to go." "Yep, that's the right way to go."

MA: So you are acting as a technical assistant in some regard for the five pilot schools?

JJ: Yeah, sort of through DaVinci.

MA: In terms of your assistance, Dana is actively seeking that. You said she would stop by on her way to work. How frequently would that happen?

JJ: Probably every three or four weeks. Sometimes it'll be two weeks in a row, other times it'll be a little while between. And we will do email or . . . the mentoring activity would help a great deal because she would say to the student, "I need you to get this done." Or "I need you to have JJ do this and give me the data." So he would come out here and say, "We have to get this fixed." And I would fix it, so . . . if we didn't have that connection as well, she would have been out quite a bit more often.

MA: So that was really an important piece of it?

JJ: Yeah, certainly a more efficient piece for her time.

MA: Well, that leads to my next set of questions, which are about students. What were your general impressions of secondary students' use of GIS?

JJ: Well the problem there is DaVinci is . . . a magnet school, and the students . . . they come with a lot of technical background to begin with so it's sort of a biased . . . example. That's not to say that I don't think secondary schools do this in general. It's not that they're not capable of using GIS . . . using GIS is a very different way of thinking. And so I found some students in the high school level have a knack and are sort of predisposed for thinking spatially. And there are others who are not.

Younger people who've had a lot more exposure to computers may pick up on the computers faster, but I mean that's just a means to the end. It's the, the *use* of GIS is the important part. You know, when you teach, you go around the room, "Why is everyone here?" I've had people say to me, "I thought I would retire without touching one of these computers." And they end up being some of the best GIS students I've ever had.

MA: Because they have the spatial understanding?

JJ: Yeah, and the skepticism.

MA: Well, talk to me about the skepticism. What's good about that?

JJ: Well, I mean, they don't just take everything for face value and punch numbers as they're supposed to. You know, they question everything. That's what you want.

   Some of the best trainees I've ever had were pilots who during other times of the year fly into hurricanes, and fly . . . I mean hazard pay sorts of job lines, who are being trained in GIS, and they always have this sort of devil-may-care attitude where they just whale away on it, and then, "Oh, look, I broke it." You know, they actually have a lot of fun. So to them even destroying a hard drive is . . . is, "So what?" when your job is to fly into the eye of a hurricane! They were very bright people, and that's just about all. These are folks who think 3-D, no doubt. 4-D.

MA: How do you then envision the future of GIS education in this community and/or in the state?

JJ: A lot of things are needed for it to work and I think more and more the tools are more widely available and the data are more and more available. But I really see the issue as being what you use it for and the problems you address. If you don't have the right problems to address with it, I don't think the educational experience is nearly as successful. But again, having the connection to folks who know how to address them is the key. I mean, you've said, "I think the partnership is incredible." I think it is. I don't think you can expect a teacher just to sort of read some books on GIS and say, "OK, we're going to use GIS to solve this community problem." That's a tough, very tough thing to do.

Given the unique circumstances of this county that is home to many employees of the USGS and other mapping agencies, JJ has described an equally unique school/partnership setting. But his discussion of the value of GIS for addressing local problems is the one that speaks highly to integrating GIS in any community. The technical assistants are out there; their agencies' missions are to provide information for community decision making. In our GIS in Education course for teachers, we required teachers to seek out community partners as technical assistants. See the resources section for guidelines on finding local GIS technical assistance.

Teacher Perspectives

The next four interviews are with the two teachers. The interviews are in the order in which I conducted them, so we'll piece the story together in that same sequence. The first is HL, the male geology teacher in the two-teacher team. Next is my friend and colleague DD, a national leader in GIS integration. Following the two teachers are first, a male student and second, a female student who exemplify their teachers' comments on the differences between male and female students' adoption of GIS.

Hal, Reflective Practitioner

MA: We're with Hal at DaVinci High School. How did you get interested in GIS?

HL: Seven years ago the rural school systems in Virginia sued the state Board of Education for inequity of funding between systems like our county. I was teaching in [another] county, over on the Kentucky border . . . They gave it *X* number of dollars to start up with and then they needed a project to do, and so teacher training was on their minds.

They had some connections here with DaVinci, and there was a group of a dozen or so of the teachers from southwest Virginia that came to DaVinci, and received training in the JEDI program—the Joint EDucation Initiative that was basically a CD-ROM set with NASA data, NOAA data, USGS data, and the software to be able to access that data.

I was in that first group that came the first summer. The next summer we had a second session here at DaVinci, and my instructor was Dana and we did GIS. Working on 286 machines and the old time-consuming DOS commands where you would literally . . . we would start a process and go home! We'd come back the next morning, and maybe over coffee and doughnuts, it would be finished!

On the upside, it introduced me to DaVinci and to the principal and the other staff members here. Four years ago, when they had an opening, they called, and said, "Would you like to come teach at DaVinci?" So I said, "Yeah, okay. I'll be there tomorrow!"

As I understand Dana's history . . . [with] DaVinci, she was basically brought in because of her strong technology skills to do something with remote sensing GIS. She has always worked GIS remote sensing into her curriculum. Now, when I came we started sharing students. We had the whole senior class.

This year, we decided that . . . the teachers would stay with their students the full year. So I just see my same one hundred and fifty students, and so when we are doing remote sensing, I'm in the remote sensing lab with them. I'm their instructor. And when we're doing ArcView, I'm the instructor.

MA: And you'd had, I guess, enough experience with GIS that you didn't feel uncomfortable moving with the kids?

HL: No, no. There was a little anxiety—always at first, and so I would practice or make sure I knew where all the data sets were and run through
the exercises and such. But after I'd given the spiel to the first class of
the day, it was okay. And I feel very comfortable at this point.

Being a school for science and technology, we . . . need to be on the
edge of things. Our principal is a visionary, and he realized that GIS
was going to be big, five or six or seven years ago, when he started looking for people like DD to come. The whole idea of being able to graphically display data and to do analysis and make the connections between
them really intrigued all of us. At the beginning, I think it was more a
toy that we did things with and said, "Okay, here's this neat technology."
We were using canned data sets and lessons from . . . whomever. Then
we began to develop some neat activities, but they didn't necessarily fit
nicely into our curriculum.

But the last two years, the curriculum, by chance or by design, has
matched the technology. And so now, GIS and remote sensing is just . . .
it's an integral part. [Now] we cannot run our curriculum without this
technology. So there was evolution there. And I think that was . . . more
our learning curve than anything else.

The [students] who have . . . truly "got" geoscience have bought
into the whole program, I think they have a very high opinion of what
we do, and have come to see the power of GIS in fact links the whole
world, environmental problems as you will. A lot of our seniors begin
the year hostile to the course, because number one, it's a required
course, and they're seniors, okay? And then number two, it does take up
a time slot when they could take yet another AP course, if they didn't
have geoscience. By this time of year, some of the kids . . . who pro-
tested the loudest have done the most work, and we've been very, very
pleased with them.

We're working toward [countywide adoption]. Of course, the
county school systems—the county schools and their teachers—are
where we were maybe five years ago. Some of the teachers, though, have
developed projects, not to the magnitude that . . . we do here, but
they'll have a six-week project. So it has, I think, a lot of good potential.
I think it's interesting that our county has chosen to implement it in the
science field, whereas I know some of our neighboring school systems
do it in social studies.

The Evolving Geosystems Course

HL: [USGS is] our primary partner, we also work closely with NASA. [Hal
and I were meeting in the school's planetarium.] We've been working

with them for three years. Most government agencies will give us all sorts of data and expertise. The EPA has been real good to us. ESRI itself could not be better to work with.

The idea at DaVinci has always been that geoscience would be the capstone course, the senior-level course. Our freshmen take biology, then chemistry, and physics as a junior, and then geoscience—the required ... the core science curriculum. And then they take all sorts of other things along the way that are of their interest. And our task was to integrate everything they had learned in those three sciences with everything that we're supposed to teach in a more traditional earth science classroom—astrology, meteorology, oceanography, geology, and ecology—and throw in a healthy dose of technology along the way. Impossible!

We only had nine months to do that. So, the course has gone through a lot of evolution since that rather ambitious beginning ... The county, from various sources of pressure, decided that what we were doing was an okay thing to do. And they were very interested in the systems approach and of course call their class the geosystems course.

Student Internship Explained

HL: As a requirement, just at DaVinci, each senior has to do what is referred to as a senior tech lab or a mentorship. And we have a dozen or so tech labs. So they have to pick one of those tech labs to do what's a yearlong project, or they will go out of the building on a mentorship with some of our business and government partners, and do the same sort of thing.

Basically, they're doing research ... maybe the most unique thing about DaVinci and the science program is that senior experience where most of the time they get a real appreciation for doing science and the constraints about doing science and the timetables and such. Something that goes on far too much [in schools] is that we [teachers] set up a lab and in ninety minutes, we go from concept to final analysis, and of course, that's not the way it works in science.

The shortest [option] would be a semester of mentorship, but most of the students—three-quarters of the students—take the yearlong tech lab option, so they're working the same project now for nine months, ten months. And that's ... that's more realistic. I'm happy with that.

MA: I spoke with [your USGS partner], and it seems that the student who is working on the mentorship with him actually provided a nice link between you all.

HL: Yes, yes, he did. This was a case where USGS had the data, but they didn't have it in the format or the size package that we needed. And we had the student power, so it was a nice ... a nice link.

I've always been a little leery of that sort of relationship, because we have had offers in the past that were just so one-sided, that we worried we were . . . getting exploited. But our county has a tremendous amount of GIS data and they've given us a great deal of it. But they have more that hasn't been digitized yet, and they have offered to let us send students out there and spend their day digitizing. Well, there's not much learning [taking place] after the first hour on a digitizing tablet, so we've declined those sorts of offers. But USGS was . . . was much more equitable.

Hal raises an interesting nuance in school/community partnership: maintaining that balance between service, learning, and mutual capacity building without the situation becoming nonproductive or exploitative of students.

Generational and Gender Issues of Learning GIS

MA: So now, to look into their learning a little bit, how do you see students learning and incorporating GIS? I'm looking at learning with GIS, gender-specific issues. And the other issues I'm kind of interested in are the generational issues.

HL: Okay. Generational . . . our students have grown up with technology and the bulk of them are not afraid of technology at all. Whereas we worried about breaking things at my age, the students have no fear at all. So they're oblivious to a lot of the concerns that we had about using technology.

There is a decided gender issue in technology at our school . . . as far as the gender issues go, [it's] decidedly biased toward males in the technology and all the upper science- and math-level courses. Computer systems lab, for example, which I think, and by all accounts of competitions and national awards, is one of the best computer systems courses—high school or university—in the nation. Our kids go out and beat . . . the MITs at the computer games and design and competitions and such. So, very, very good program—one of the best at DaVinci. And the ratio is maybe 12:1, 14:1 boy to girl.

In our tech labs, we see females gravitating towards the more traditional female sciences and things like biotechnology instead of robotics, for instance. So we notice that in our classrooms as well. And it's certainly not because that one or the other sex is more talented, or they wouldn't be here in the first place.

So that's something that we're grappling with as a faculty, is why is this and what can we do to make it . . . I'm very personally getting involved with it because I have a daughter, and so I think maybe I'm a little more aware of it than the average faculty person. I have taken some gender equity courses and have served on several committees around the building just to try to see what's going on, and I make it a point to talk to my girls and say, "Why aren't you taking this course?" Or "Why are you taking this course?" So there is . . . that difference in the technology.

Dana and I have addressed [this issue] by insisting that we not have all-male groups or all-female groups. Even as we pair up or team up to do computer assignments, like the first quarter, we said, "Okay, you can choose your own person to work with." The second quarter, it has to be same sex; the third quarter, it has to be different sex; and the fourth quarter, I don't know what we did—somebody you hadn't worked with before, or something like that, to do our best to give equal access to the technology.

The boys are much more familiar with technology in general and they do grab the mouse every time, and of course, the person who has the mouse has the control. And so it's a struggle to get the mouse in the right hands all the time. So that's . . . that's . . . that's a little tough.

My reason for asking about generational and gender issues was to consider the students' social context for learning GIS. The generational advantage may be divided by the gender gap, and this is a compelling reason to integrate GIS technology in social studies as compared to science classes. While Delany teachers saw similar patterns in the U.S. middle school, the Canadian teacher observation differed. This may be due to the context of the class into which GIS is integrated—geography vs. the sciences, where there have been documented differences.

HL: The kids like ArcView. It's a real intuitive thing software-wise to use. Again, they need to be exposed earlier to the idea of this graphical representation to visualize stuff, to see the connections between things. In general, our students are very poor geographers.

Integrating Historical Data with Student-Gathered Data: Field Research

MA: I take it there was a major field component to this course, and I'd like you to talk about the relationship between the fieldwork and the GIS and how you see that balancing.

HL: As a field geologist—I mean that's my training and I worked as a professional geologist for a number of years, and came kind of late to the education scene formally—maps are just a tool that geologists use all the time. It's the way that we represent data. So, graphically visualizing data has never been a problem for me. I'm very at home with that. Very committed to having a hands-on, experiential science program. As a geologist, that has to include a field component.

So, it was important, as we designed the project and literally built our curriculum around the project, that it have that field component. We searched for different problems that we could tackle that would meet many criteria, but one of which was, it had to have a field component in it. And we said, "Well, let's talk about the relationship of urban imperviousness to stream flow." It was a good fit with the technology, because we were using satellite imagery and image processing tools to see where impervious areas were and where they had increased over time. We were getting historical stream flow data from the USGS' archives, and we were getting historical precipitation data from NOAA's archives.

So we visited streams several times. Our students did minor water quality tests. DD insisted that I not go overboard on the water quality or the different parameters that we introduced into the project this year. But we did lots of the physical parameters of the streams—we ran transects and drew cross sections and calculated discharge both at current levels, and then projected what storm discharge would be based on the physical characteristics of the streambed.

There was also a field component in the ground truthing and the satellite data, so each student chose a point—basically a pixel that had been classified as some sort of a land class from low-density residential to park land or agricultural or quarry, whatever—and then they went into the field, found the point, and observed what was there.

MA: Do you do the field component all through the year?

HL: Pretty much all through the year. We begin with some basic fieldwork just in maps, for instance, in the fall, we did our ground truthing in the second and third quarters, and we did our stream studies in the third and fourth quarters. We have found over the years that the sooner you get them in the field, the better the year goes.

So we are tinkering with the sequencing of the little units that we teach. It's hard—how do you take them out into the field to collect steam data before that you teach them something about maps, before that you teach them something about streams, so there's a little push and shove, and we try to make things fit. So it's not perfect yet, but each year gets a little closer to what works.

MA: I guess I should ask you about time, because I guess the practical questions that teachers would have are about how you do fieldwork, how do you get the time, are you on a block schedule, or, how do you work that part of things?

HL: DaVinci is on a block schedule. We have an anchor day on Mondays that we meet all eight periods, and then we alternate even and odd periods on a block schedule the rest of the week. So . . .

MA: So the class meets . . .

HL: Three days a week. We have them forty-five minutes on Mondays, and then an hour and a half on two other days of the week. So all of our fieldwork would be done on those block days. We try very hard to only use our ninety minutes of time to do fieldwork, so as not to infringe on the other faculty. That's a big problem at DaVinci. So much goes on so quickly that if a kid misses a ninety-minute block period, they're forever making up work. So we try to be sensitive to that. One of the advantages that we have is that we're teaching seniors, and they can drive. So transportation to the field is not a concern for us. So teaching at the upper level—junior/senior level—that is a plus. Again, our students are incredibly responsible, so we're not too concerned about them not showing up at the field site. We always check in at the beginning of the period, and arrange car pools so everybody has a ride, and then we check when we get there, and we check when we leave, and finally when we come back. All of those sort of administrative things to cover anything that might happen. But, we by and large trust the students and they respond to that trust. They earn it. So we do go into the field quite often . . . the goal would be several times in a quarter. One of the things that works in our favor in our county is the county owns and has developed as county park land most of the stream valleys, so it's a great match for what we do. And the county was very willing to give us a permit to be on their land and to allow us to take samples, soil and rock and water, and whatever that we needed.

Repeated visits are where you can begin to collect quality data. The first few visits are just get-acquainted visits. We asked our students to draw a site map of this location. And then the next time, let's take some basic stream measurements, and let's do a profile. Then we go back again, and let's do two profiles in different locations. So they keep building on it, and we're building data at the same time, but fully realizing that the last data they collect is the best we're going to get. But the repeated visits are very important. I think the repetition gets lost a lot in [the regular] hectic education schedule [where] we run a lab, we grade it, we go on to something else. [In the capstone], we don't have to run a lab and grade it—we *do* it, grade it, redesign it, do it again. And that's sort of the way that we approach the field experience. Absolutely.

Tolerating Ambiguity—Students and Teachers

HL: At the beginning of the year, one thing that we had to battle was that we divided up into teams, and we tried to match up the skills each team would need with various students. So we had teams of six or [so] working [together]. And between all the classes that DD and I teach, that gave us thirty-some groups to work with and they were all saying, "We've got thirty-some groups doing the exact same project, we'll have thirty-some answers exactly the same." We said, "Don't worry about that." When it comes up to presentation and paper time, no group has exactly the same answer. So that was a nice learning experience for them was that, yes, you can make a lot of different things out of the same data set. Intuitively we know what's right, but the final word we'll get on June 3rd when we do the presentation and we present the findings.

I was able to return to DaVinci for the students' presentations at their impressive county complex auditorium. The student presentations were sophisticated and direct. County agents, USGS scientists, and legislators questioned the students, who all stood behind their data with confidence. The students weren't in the least intimidated or shy about telling nationally powerful leaders how poorly their national stream gauge program had fared over the years and how it had hampered their analysis.

Reflections on Teaching with GIS

HL: We've contributed greatly to the learning process of the students. It involved a yearlong study, a yearlong laboratory, if you will, experiment rather than a ninety-minute one, and they see what really happens. Well, they're collecting all this great data and they're seeing, boy, this is tough. This is not black and white! I can't come up with this equation or this one point and know for sure that this is right or not. That's something to think about in using GIS and teaching it. It's a pretty big departure, too. The answers aren't always black and white, because now we can visualize them so many different ways it opens up too many possibilities to their minds. The kids are very bright here, but they're still teenagers, and they don't have the intellectual maturity that a JJ does after X number of years of research. So I think that's a good thing about what we do in our program.

MA: That's neat. Well, also, I think maybe one of the reasons is that curve that teachers have to go through, because it's a big leap of faith to say there isn't a right answer.

HL: That's a huge leap of faith. It's not what teachers have been willing to say in the past. That's the first thing I say: "I don't know. Let's see if we can figure it out." I've always done that and I'm certainly not going to stop when I get here, when I'm probably the least intelligent person in my classroom!

I look at them over maturity and experience [which] is about all I've got on the people around here. So, yeah, there's so many things that we don't know. Just admitting that to a student, that takes a special person, or one that's maybe secure enough in what they do know to admit what they don't know. So that's different for the kids, too. And this idea that maybe there's not an answer, and even though we've worked for thirty-six weeks on this problem—that we still don't know what the answer is. But, in defense of our little project, this year, we actually have come to some clear closure. Yes, we didn't find *the* answer, but we're seeing trends of collected data, and we had an idea of what is happening. Just because we can't prove it, the kids are beginning to recognize that we don't have enough data to prove it. Boy, that's a big one!

When all was said and done, we only ended up with what I considered three data points to base this whole study on. And so I've got a kid that's fitting a curve to three points and saying this is the answer. Well, he's not so sure now that that's the answer. That's been good, very, very good. And they have learned the limitations of data. Our county has fifty-three stream monitoring stations, but only two of them are currently operating. And when we went to match up time frames when we had precipitation data and stream flow data and satellite coverage, out of those fifty-three, we found three that fit, OK? Well, that was a shock to them. And the first thing they want to do is to call their congressman and say they needed more money! It was a nice thing to see happen. "Yeah, this is important. We need to fund these monitoring stations." So—a lot of good through the project. And there's no way that we could do this project or anything else that we had planned in the future without a visualization tool, and GIS is it. It's wonderful. So much potential here. We're just scratching the surface.

Students Contributing to the Community

HL: That was one of the biggest things that we contributed to USGS is that they had never ground truthed their classification system. [As] JJ put it—and this is how things happen in government—someone asked the director how accurate their classification system was. He had no idea— he made up a number. He said, "It's 85 percent accurate," and that's the standard they have been using for years now. They had no idea! So now we can tell them with some certainty what their accuracy is. Not with great certainty, but it's sure better than making up a number! So that was another field component of the project. GIS was, of course, just imperative to data analysis. We had to have it.

The Social Studies Connection

Here's the major potential social studies component. In this particular county, students could have followed through with urging their legislator-parents or neighbors to rectify the faulty stream gauge stations. Students in many areas would clearly want to bring their findings to light in the community. Depending upon its polity (town meeting, city council, county government), they could affect policy. In all of the U.S. classes I visited, there was some sort of public presentation of the GIS data. When students have the opportunity to effect real change in communities, we have fulfilled our mission in social studies to develop students as participants in a democracy.

On the Future of GIS in Schools

MA: So I guess that kind of brings me to two questions: What are the long-term benefits of including GIS in a curriculum and then how do you envision GIS in education in the future?

HL: Well, we have some very immediate benefits to many of our students. Each year, we place students in summer jobs doing GIS. And . . .

MA: Where do they go, mostly?

HL: Mostly to government and industry. One of the kids that we placed earliest this year is working with a defense contractor who has been given the contract to produce a worldwide unexploded-land-mine map, okay. And so we sent a kid over to interview for a summer position, and literally, this kid is now running the project because he knows more about ArcView and GIS than anybody at the contractor does! That's a very typical thing. Not bragging on us too much, but when our kids leave the classroom, they can do pretty well. They can do just about anything that an average company or government body would want them to do with GIS.

So there's immediate benefits, and I'm quick to point out the capabilities that regardless of what they're going to do in life, if they have the knowledge of ArcView in particular, or just the graphic visualization in general, that they're going to do a better job at it. So, as one of the long-term benefits to the students, they are going to be more and more exposed to this sort of way of analyzing data, so they're a giant leap ahead of most other people. Of course the possibilities in our curricular areas are unlimited, too. And as many schools have chosen to start in the social sciences, you know, tremendous opportunities there.

So, I can't imagine education in the future without GIS. I know it will be . . . it is a mainstay of what we'll do here. Speaking as my scientific half, I know it's the greatest thing since toast to do with data, because . . . making a hand-drawn geologic map of an area [with] only one layer at a time? [Compared to] now I can have as many layers as I want in 3-D! Oh, this is tremendous, what's going to be possible. And possible in our classroom here, because . . . the computer technology is cheap enough to run it, the learning curve on ArcView is easy enough to work with it, and they just keep adding all those wonderful extensions to it. *Spatial Analyst* [an ArcView extension program] we introduced this year, *3-D Analyst* we'll introduce next year. I just can't wait! Such an exciting place to be—all around. But the possibilities for education are tremendous. Really, really, exciting.

Dana and I . . . we like what we do here, we like the kids we work with, and for the first year since I've been here—this is my fourth year at DaVinci—we have a curriculum that works. It is an integrated curriculum. We have integrated science and technology in our program. And now, all those things that we couldn't do before, we can. We can make the connections between the fieldwork, which is the part that I love, and the technology. And they each complement each other so well. That's exciting.

Teacher Criteria for a Capstone Geosystems Course

Hal described the most important criteria he and Dana used to select an appropriate problem as the focus for the yearlong student inquiry:

HL: Well one of the things that we do with all of our projects is that we have basically four criteria they have to meet:

  • Number 1, *It has to be a real problem*—it has to be doing real science for an existing problem, for a need that exists. We're not just going to pull it out of thin air.

  • Number 2, *It has to be local,* just for logistics, so the kids . . . it has to be something in their lives, where they live, something that we could physically get to and get back from and collect data.

  • [Number 3] *It has to be an area that we have some expertise in*—at least enough to get started.

  And then finally,

  • *It has to be a question that we feel we could answer.* Something that we have the resources to do and that includes resources of time and materials, etc.

So if it meets those four criteria, we look at it. And that leads us to lots of different places. We start with maybe the soil conservation people who lead us to EPA who lead us to some other Virginia group that said, "Oh, you need to talk to JJ Jones." It just goes around, and finally we make the connection.

Dana: A GIS Innovator

Now we move to the interview with Dana, which took place in her kitchen. Her neighborhood is adjacent to a national preserve—in one of the few parts of the county that has retained its rural character since its population explosion.

MA: How did you become interested in GIS?

DD: I was teaching earth science at [a] high school in Virginia, and they called me up to come and interview at DaVinci High School for Science and Technology. And when I went to interview . . . the principal was trying to get some of the new technologies that were—kind of revitalizing earth science—he was trying to get some of those into their geoscience curriculum, which was a senior-level culminating science course that combined everything the kids knew about biology and physics and chemistry their senior year. And he wanted the new technology, geographic information systems and remote sensing and if possible, modeling and the use of Internet in this course. Now, that's the first time I'd heard of GIS. And he asked me if I would have any problem with that, and I said no.

MA: Wait a minute! Back up. Had you ever done—applied technology before?

DD: No! I had a Macintosh. My background was I had worked with Apple II GSs and some Probeware—computer-based lab-type thing. And then I had a Macintosh that I had done some image processing on with the interplanetary images, using an image and then I'd done Hypercard. So that was my background, and when I went to DaVinci it was all like 286 DOS machines, and they had—on one machine—[Clark University's] Idrisi, which was a raster-based GIS. And I started messing around with it and reading their training manual—which is a really, really good training manual—and I just kind of understood it. I mean, the minute I saw it and knew we were going to layer stuff and reclass and query, it kind of clicked.

So I started playing around with Idrisi, and the first year there—the first year I was at DaVinci—I just played around on the machine. The second year, we got enough copies of Idrisi that we put it on twelve really low-end 286 machines. And that year, we cycled the whole senior class through my lab, and when I said we did GIS, we did it with very generic-type data sets. We did all the stuff that Idrisi had on there, which was a data set from Massachusetts. So with remote sensing, we did GIS for the strict purpose of only doing GIS remote sensing. We were not in any way involved in any kind of problem. We graduated a class then that knew what remote sensing was, knew what GIS was, and knew what the Internet was. They knew exactly what it was, but they had not had applications or anything.

Initiating the GIS/Geosystems Capstone Course

DD: Next year they gave us a lab of Pentiums. And from that time on, every-thing just kind of took off exponentially, because I had been trying to run ArcView on a 486, and it was ArcView 2.0 and it was just not good. When I got the Pentiums, and we installed ArcView—I think it was 2.1—then we kind of like expanded a lot because it just got our capabil-ities going. At the same time I had contacted our county—the GIS department—and had gone over there. And they said that they would give our county schools the database for the county. So they cut us . . . they cut us one CD . . . no, they actually brought it to me on Zip, and I took it to our technology people, and they cut a CD and made a CD for all the teachers in the county.

Now, at the same time, I have kind of always been committed to the fact that the seniors' course was not supposed to be something that the kids got out of the textbook, but it was supposed to be some problem that they were involved in where they were not [just] reading about sci-ence, but actually *doing* science.

Necessary Components

DD: There were a couple of parameters that I wanted to have for a school-based project.

- I wanted it to involve GIS.
- I wanted it involve remote sensing.
- I wanted it to involve the Internet.
- I wanted it to involve some typical earth science project or geoscience problem that would traditionally be taught, like hydrology or geology.
- I also wanted it to be something that we could do some fieldwork in. Now, I had done a lot of things like fires of Yellowstone, Mississippi flood, etc., etc., but when you're doing GIS and remote sensing, you're always trying to find maps and everything to go along with what you're doing. So I wanted something that dealt with our county.

Our fourth year, we got involved with a project where I probably made every mistake that a person makes going into a new GIS, which was . . . "The more data I had, the better it was going to be." So I had probably twenty-five layers of data. I had no idea what I was trying to look for. If you would have asked any kid they would probably not have been able to state for you the entire purpose of the project. So, while we learned a lot about GIS, I don't think we learned too much about the science of the whole thing. So this year . . . Kids collected data—kids collected soil data, the kids collected EPA science, the kids collected . . . I mean, if a group of kids didn't have something to do, they did another layer. The missing link here was that we never got anybody connected together.

The next year, which brings us up to this year, is when I seriously felt like I had to get a handle on the fact that we weren't getting anywhere! And I've always had a really close relationship with USGS. Now before I got to DaVinci, before I was ever there, this guy that I worked with at USGS had given a workshop to a group of teachers. But I had stayed in touch with him, and he had always been really good. If I was having technical problems, he'd answer a problem and had given us additional info and various things. So I went out and met with him and said I wanted a project that involved traditional science, something I was interested in. Something that involved the kids' own neighborhood, where they lived. And something that involved satellite imagery.

We kicked it around a while . . . and he came up with the fact that number one, any type of satellite imagery that's classified, they didn't have any statistics on how accurate it was. That was the first part of the project that was going to be a land cover assessment piece. And the second part of the project was, as an impervious area of our county changes, does it do anything to stream flow in the area's streams? A little watershed hydrology—and we both agreed—and he agreed to keep me in check—that we would have two variables—stream flow and imperviousness. And if we even tried to put another variable in there, each one of us was going to slap the other one!

Ground Truth

DD: Okay, the first part of the project was to ground truth or to see how accurate remote sensing satellite imagery would be if we were going to use it in any kind of a GIS project. In other words, was something classified from a LANDSAT satellite going to be 50 percent accurate? Now

I'll be frank with you, I thought this was going to take us about a day and a half! It was an incredibly complicated experience.

First of all, I had it in my head that the kids were going to ground truth a point where they lived, and this was partly because of the teacher and the mother in me, I didn't want the kids driving around [the entire] county. Once we decided to do that though, and I ran this by JJ. He immediately said that that was not going to be a random selection of points. And any of my seniors that had had statistics didn't like that either . . . I still made the kids pick a point closest to their house even [though] that makes it unrandom. Having had that assigned, their assignment then was to go out and map on a paper map—a tax map—an area thirty meters in diameter and one hundred meters in diameter . . . But what they *actually* had to do is make some sort of judgment as to what the nine-hundred square-meter area— what the satellite would classify it as.

DaVinci's USGS partner, JJ, had wanted to maintain statistical randomness in the study area to assure its validity. In a raster-based map, square pixels are assigned a specific color or greyscale value according to what was remotely sensed. The sensing, based on heat reflected from the earth's surface, can be affected by interference such as heat bouncing off of reflective surfaces (think about Beltway traffic), atmospheric conditions such as smog, or other factors. When areas were ground truthed, students went to the *actual* location and photographed and mapped the conditions there. Impervious surfaces could include roads, parking lots, rooftops, buildings, outcrops of rock. Permeable surfaces would include lawns, fields, forest, swales, medians, or open areas of any kind that could absorb precipitation rather than shed it as runoff that could potentially cause flooding. As development reduces permeable surfaces, flood hazards and pollution become more concentrated.

Dana continues,

DD: I had the kids design their own protocols as to how they were going to go about ground truthing this data, and that was probably . . . that was probably one of the adrenaline highs of the whole year, because I didn't know what I wanted and I gave them . . . not specific, not structured directions, and they—each group—came up with a little something different. So that was really, really good. So that was one of the highs, was having them design this protocol. We then took the best things from each one to kind of write out the other one. So after we did that, then the kids classified it according to Anderson's Classification, which is a typical land cover classification done by USGS.* So anyway, they classified them, and then we had to statistically compare them to see how accurate the satellite image was to even see whether or not it would be useful in studies to do this kind of thing.

Okay, once we did that, and you see, there was a tremendous amount of statistical math in here that we struggled with, and if I had not had kids that had had statistics, it would have been difficult. There is a certain number of points that you have to ground truth to get a certain confidence level . . . each group had to do their own error matrix of the data. That's the power of the GIS, because we could just say, "Show me where the ground truth points matched up with the other points," and they could statistically give it to you. If you were going to do this by hand, it would probably have been a nightmare. So this is one of the ways that the GIS was really worthwhile.

Community-Based Environmental History

DD: At the same time, one of my students was working with JJ Jones in a mentorship project. And his mentorship was classifying [image] data from the '80s and '90s for us to compare . . . each pixel covers a much broader range. And he classified these two sets of data and gave it to us, and then of course we're able to query out, like, "Show us high intensity, show us low intensity, show us wooded residential." And knowing how much imperviousness he said each type of land had, we were able to calculate the different watersheds from the '80s and '90s, and tabulate how much it had changed and then make our own watershed index by percentage, showing the watersheds that had changed the most imperviousness. And it came out that, as you would think, the ones right around . . . the national airport, they don't have much percentage

---

* The "Anderson Classification" is a land cover classification system developed by the USGS in cooperation with NASA, the Natural Resource Conservation Service (NRCS), the Association of American Geographers (AAG), and the International Geographical Union (IGU). "The nine general categories of the classification system are: 1. Urban or built-up land; 2. Agricultural land; 3. Rangeland; 4. Forest land; 5. Water; 6. Wetland; 7. Barren land; 8. Tundra; 9. Perennial snow and ice. These categories are further divided into subcategories that convey additional information about the cover type. This standardized classification allows comparisons of land cover and land use to be made between different parts of the country. UNESCO, part of the United Nations, has developed a worldwide land cover classification scheme which is generally convertible into Anderson classes, although some merging or splitting may be required in some landscapes. Other classification approaches have been developed and used across the country, although many are based on the Anderson system." From <http://www.geography.wisc.edu/sco/maps/landcover.html>.

of change, because . . . they were already built up anyway. But out in the western part of the county . . . and out towards Dulles, then they drastically change because in the last ten years, so much of the land has been built up. So we were actually able to calculate how much the land had changed.

Now, the science of this comes into play here, because number one, when we started this whole thing off, I don't think any of us had had too much background of imperviousness, and we defined imperviousness as being if it's paved or if it's a rooftop. So I had the kids go out and do a photo album of impervious surfaces. They did photos of things that are being done in the metropolitan area to help imperviousness, like the silt fences . . . those silt fences that help erosion and cluster development that leaves open spaces, and they took pictures of erosion and retention ponds, just because I wanted them to be aware of what was helping and what was around them. So that was one of the things we were doing in conjunction with all this remote sensing.

With GIS I actually have just a couple of activities . . . I get them to using ArcView very, very quickly. They make a map of the state, certain things that tell them how to convert the shapefiles, etc. They have to map where they live, of course, the street in their area. And then we have Spatial Analyst, so we can proof the satellite data. So we did various little activities and you would be amazed at how little we spent time-wise on just the basics of the software, because the goal was here to get the software and get the technology kind of entwined with what we were trying to do with the science. So it kind of linked up really good.

This is the first year—the very first year—that I can tell you that I was not just teaching GIS, that we were actually using GIS and using remote sensing to solve a problem that we selected and wanted to know something about. The hard part about this is that your curriculum kind of goes in spurts and valleys, because you figure something out and you just have like a thrust forward, but then you like get hung up and it . . . you have downtime. So it's not like doing a curriculum that you know exactly what's going to happen every day out of a book, it's like ups and downs.

MA: But that's more like real science.

DD: Yes. I think . . . I think the nature of our school—it being a lab school and a magnet school—the kids are more tolerant of this. I think in a normal high school . . . I do not think they need as much structure as they have, but I think they need more than what we've got at our school. Because our kids are very patient if we can't figure it out right away.

Collaborative Co-construction of Instruction with Students

Here I take issue with my friend Dana's opinion that students in a school like DaVinci are more tolerant of the ups and downs of using GIS. Based on my experience in a technical high school where students were—to use Howard Gardner's multiple intelligences typology—more kinesthetic learners, meaning they were hands-on learners, I see the skills as utterly transferable and *not* limited to one student population or another. When at my school we conducted an archeological dig over a three-year period, students responded exactly as Dana's had—they respected the ambiguities of doing "authentic" research, primarily because they knew it was the real thing—it was messy and uncertain, and we were constantly in a state of problem solving.

MA: While we're talking about students, how would you characterize the skills of the students participating? How were students selected? Do most come from homes with computers and how would you characterize their prior computer skills?

DD: Our kids are smart. That's the first thing. Now their computer skills are strange. Some of them are geniuses, and know more about computers than I would ever want to know. And some of them can barely tell you the difference between the C and the A drive. Two of the girls did not have good computer skills, and they've done great work for me. But they've plugged at it … it's easy to get overpowered when you're around kids that are as good as some of our kids are on computers. So they've done . . . they've probably gotten more out of it than anybody, because they've plugged away by themselves and kind of developed not only GIS skills, but computer skills as they go along. I would say most of our kids have computers in their home. We're not talking about kids that don't know how to use the mouse or don't know how to do file management— they know all of that.

Addressing Gender Issues of Learning with GIS

DD: So, I would say as a general rule, my boys are better than girls at it. And I try to get my girls in it, but nine times out of ten, if you see kids who are doing GIS with me, it'll be boys. So . . . I have a plan that I make them do. The first nine weeks, they get to sit with whoever they want to. The second nine weeks, they have to sit same sex, so boys have to sit with boys, and girls have to sit with girls. That is the worst nine weeks I have because the boys are . . . they are . . . they fight with each other, because they both want to use the mouse. But if you have a boy and girl together, the boy will always use the mouse and the girl will write. And then, the third nine weeks, they have to sit with somebody they'd never sat with before, and then the fourth nine weeks, I'll let them . . . go back and sit with whoever they want to. But it's not good if you let them sit with the same person the whole year, because they . . . one will work the computer and one will write. So it's good if you kind of mix them up.

MA: What kinds of preparatory skills or activities do you design to frame the introduction of GIS?

DD: I try to tell them what GIS is supposed to be—a scientific visualization tool that goes from okay, let's not look at data in a spreadsheet, let's map it and get some kind of visual picture of it, and that you're seeing the relationship between layers of variables. I've tried always to teach the software separate from what I wanted to do with it. In fact, my activity that teaches with GIS is to . . . pick any state in the United States, other than Hawaii, and make a map of the counties, of the rivers, the streams. Of all of those counties, you have to show me the counties with the lowest population in red, you have to make a layout. Has nothing to do with anything—it is strictly software manipulation. They have to do point data and show me the equator and the prime meridian.

There's a lot of people saying that you need specific lessons of GIS. I think you need specific lessons to get people started, but after that . . . I can't do everything with specific lessons. Because if you do, you take away the one thing you want the kids to do, which is to think of what they want the software to do to solve the problem. Sometimes I don't think there's enough specific lessons about GIS. I don't think what we want is a book of lessons on GIS. In fact, those books that are published that have ArcView lessons—those are fine. Those are fine to do, but then to have the kids solve the problems using imperviousness—it's two different things.

Addressing Generational Issues in Learning with GIS

DD: Now one thing about kids that's funny is that once they understand this point data and these attributes of mapping it, they've got it. I mean once they understand what we're trying to do, it's just like they can map anything. And most kids that I work with understand that by the second day. Adults, I don't know. Adults struggle with the software so much, I don't know whether sometimes we get the whole thing. I mean, one of the things we have the kids do when we're studying earthquakes is bring in the earthquake data, and we have them bring in twenty years of earthquake data, and they have the month, the year, the day, the time, the depth, and the magnitude. And the kids say to me, "Mrs. D, I think more earthquakes occur during the springtime." As long as they know they have the frequency of earthquakes and they have the time on it, and they can compare the two, I'm fine. I mean, why do you want to know that?

The other thing is that people don't understand about this GIS stuff—I've got a lab, I've got eleven machines, and I'm teaching 150 kids a day. So you have to have an archived data set on your machine. And then the kids have to save every day, each in a directory of their own, each class, what they did. That's a pretty heavy load on your hard drives. So you can't go messin' around with these huge data sets. I mean, we can barely do our county. If we had anything bigger than that, it would be too much. And that's because you want all the kids to have the experience of doing it! I don't have enough resources to get four different problems going.

A Completely Different Pedagogy

DD: But there's never that good old downtime when you were just answering the good old thirty questions in the book. It's not like that—it's not like you're going to show that great long movie! And I don't know how many times I have to say to the kids, "I don't know," but it's a lot! If people heard me, they'd think, does this woman know anything?

So the whole style of teaching changes from, not, "Let me show you how to do this," but it's, "Let's see, between all of us, if we can figure this out." It's a completely different pedagogy than I'm used to. And some people have a really hard time with that. I would say that I don't think it's really the technology of GIS, it's the whole teaching style that you do with GIS. It's not the computer. It's not the interface. It's the fact that it's not canned, and it's real life and the data doesn't do what it's supposed to do—nothing does what it's supposed to do! (*She smiles.*)

MA: But you *are* doing real research.

DD: Well, we're certainly trying, and you have to make decisions and you have to argue about it. The bottom line is, just like this project—the kids are saying, "Mrs. D, we're not done," and I'm saying, "It doesn't matter whether we're not done or not—the presentation's on June 3rd!" That's the way life is. So that's kind of problematic.

The other way I've been blessed is that I have people to talk to about it. If you were doing this in a vacuum, it would be impossible. Now the one thing I can see GIS doing is—we've been talking about doing interdisciplinary science for now fifteen years—that GIS can help to integrate statistics, physics, hydrology, geology, English, and everything on the map, and hang it onto one thing. The GIS will give you a place to store and a way to display it.

At the end of the chapter, I'll review Dana's important reflections on the teaching of the capstone course. Just how well their students have internalized the processes, functions, and critical perspectives ranges predictably. In the following interviews with students, we'll see the widest range I encountered among the DaVinci students.

Student Perspectives

Regardless of where on the learning continuum these two students fall, I think you'll agree that their learning was enhanced by the capstone experience. The first interview is with a male student; the second, a female. Both of the students were Caucasian seniors.

Jeff's Critical Perspective

Jeff: I thought it [learning with GIS] was very intuitive, actually, because most of the stuff was computer based, so most of it is being able to manipulate the data and being able to understand it conceptually—what you're looking at. Because if you just look at numbers and whatnot, you can get confused. I thought it was very intuitive in terms of saying, "This is how I can solve this problem—by looking at this and taking away all of these other variables and solving this problem."

And it was helpful, I mean, in fact I got a job. (*Chuckles.*) It's not using GIS to do anything geography-related but it's being able to use the software to manipulate large amounts of data over the nation, because it's a radio tower company and they build and they buy up radio towers and they want to know—"Where shall I build this tower to make the most money?" And that has a lot to do with elevation, it has a lot to do with population density and all that stuff, so it's essentially taking all the same skills and using it make a profit margin.

MA: So your knowledge of GIS was something that they wanted.

Jeff: Yeah, especially my knowledge of ArcView, because they have—they use a competitor—MapInfo—that's similar-based software—it's vector-based software.

Developing Analytical Skills

Jeff: I think the biggest thing about using those skills is honing your analytical skills, first of all, how you're getting the data—like what's happening from the perspective of—if this is a spectral response or whatever—what is this? And if I get that sort of response, what does that mean? And then once you get what it means, then, how did it get represented to me when I look at it? And then being able to combine those three is I think the most important thing. That you can look at one aspect and still understand where it's all coming from. Because if you look at an image in Idrisi, it looks pretty, but you have to understand that that's a representation of some sort of numerical data, and that the colors . . . before I was involved with the geoscience at all, I remember wondering, "Why did they choose the colors that way?" It really doesn't make any difference, it's just to illustrate the difference, and I think [recognizing that is] the biggest skill.

MA: Mm-hm, so the interpretation.

In fact, here, the student is analyzing the data *behind* the map. His understanding of the map as simply a representation, coupled with the ability to interpret and manipulate the data in a variety of ways, indicates a sophisticated and critical synthesis.

Jeff: It's also a skill to be able to learn the software and be able to manipulate the software and to change the data yourself so that you can go farther than just what's given to you.

In our project we used GIS to—we got spectral response from the imperviousness of our county and essentially we used all this data to— I mean we learned basic fundamentals about all these things first—like we learned the different vector-based software, the raster-based software, but we also took this specific project that we were working on and did a lot of analysis with the software, like being able to produce a statistically feasible study by choosing so many random points. And then we would take it and we'd have to re-project everything so that it would match up correctly. Then we'd have to say, "Oh, well we've got an error matrix here that says this is this percent correct. Then, what do we do if it's that percent correct? Well, then what's correct [and what isn't]?"

So then we have to look at it and say—then we have to draw a correlation between one set of data over another set of data. Does imperviousness over a span of time have any affect over peak stream flow over a span of time? And it turns out that, well—mechanically, you'd think this is all you can do—it's difficult to do, but we've gotten to know the software a lot better, so we've been able to analyze massive amounts of information a lot better.

It's like hypothesis testing. You're taking a hypothesis of something that might happen, or might be true, and you're taking lots and lots of streams of data and you're saying, "Oh, well, is there any way that we can project a sort of correlation?" It's not like you have an x/y where you're dealing with one variable—you're dealing with millions of variables, so you're incorporating a lot more into your study. So that's why it becomes a lot more complicated and that's why it takes so long to process all that information and to be able to come out with any real strong correlations.

Integrating the *Actual* Field Experiences

Jeff: And the ground truthing too was very important. That's why I was saying that knowing each part of the steps—like each step along the way—like knowing that if this an error of omission or an error of commission—then, what is it doing? Then actually going out to the point and seeing what it could be doing—oh—[the satellite's] classifying this half the road and half the grass—Oh, well, that's not water! Then you start understanding those things.

We did some fieldwork for the peak stream flow to go out to measure the velocity—we did a lot of stream geology, like figuring out just background information like what happens when it reaches full-bank discharge, and what does that mean, and why the measurements can be so skewed, and what parts of the data you can actually use to make some sort of correlation.

On "Growing Up Digital"

Jeff: I've used computers for most of my life. I've taken a computer science course, I've been involved in journalistic—not just word processing, but the whole—layout and all that stuff. I've sort of grown up on the whole Windows-based mentality. I think a lot of the people in this school are used to having a computer in the home. Well, we've had a computer all my life. We got a decent computer before my freshman year. But I've always known the logic behind it because my dad is an engineer and he works a lot of those things so I think a lot of it's come from what my family setting is, too.

Not to mention the fact that during my four years here, I've become very dep—not *dependent* on it, but I use a computer a lot just to do everyday stuff—research, my whole tech project was a lot of coordination, a lot of communication, a lot of using the computer, so . . .

I guess what surprised me the most was the amount of actual solid data that we have. It surprised me the different kinds of data our county had access to. Our county had a good model, so we were lucky. [But] a lot of stuff is *not* that great—you'd think that the local officials or whatever—that we'd have the—peak stream gauge stations. We used USGS images, county stream gauge data, and doing the ground truthing, we used GPS.

The student is alluding to the data issues raised in Chapter 7. His recognition of the garbage in/garbage out issues demonstrates sophisticated critical thinking. His ability to critique the data the county has could only have come from a firsthand experience of its limitations. Understanding the data behind the map represents a higher order of analysis.

Jeff: We've done two presentations in school and in order to get my job, I had to explain to my boss what my project was and what my role was in the project. So I had to prove to him how what I learned in the imperviousness project could be related to what he had to do.

To me it looks a lot harder than it actually is. I mean our whole project was based on, "This whole area is being paved over—what impact will that have on the county? " So it's sort of the scientific method applied to a commonplace problem.

Claire on Combining Multiple Applications with GIS

There is a decided difference in the tone of the preceding male student and the following female student's responses. The differences highlight teacher Hal's concerns about gender differentiation in adopting technology. Claire's image of herself in the community was much more maplike than any of the other students' representations.

Claire: Well, basically, I drew a map of my life, and I have a key—the school, different religious organizations and activities, the animal shelter where I volunteer. This is my pathetic representation of our county. I see it all the time on ArcView and GIS, so I guess I should be able to draw it by now.

Right off the top, [GIS is] software for mapping. It's not only mapping and locations, but image processing, like we have satellite imagery from LANDSAT of our county. What I thought was really neat was when we overlaid the satellite imagery with some man-made maps and you can tell how accurate your satellite imagery is—and how accurate your man-made map is when you overlay them. If you need a certain type of theme, like a schools theme or streets in the county or rivers, [they can be added].

What helps me to learn is playing with the software. I'm not a computer person, so once Mrs. D showed me how to play with the software—how to "get" themes and how to add them to my view, then it was a lot easier for me. Playing with the software really helped—just, "Gee—I wonder what this does?" She gave us an activity to learn how to use it that wasn't graded, and that was really helpful.

To [incorporate] data, we mostly used Excel. I learned a lot about Excel, to use the language, make fields and charts. We saved some data from an html file [from the Web] and then imported it into Excel. There were literally thousands of data points we needed, and that was just for one stream. ArcView we used to located the streams in the county. When we ground truthed our points, we used ArcView to integrate [it with] our county [GIS] information.

I've learned how to manipulate Windows and using the software, Windows, email, attachments, and that in conjunction with each other to get the job done—Excel, Word, my email system, the Internet, and ArcView to be able to get the documents together [for] the project.

One of the things I thought was neat was being able to download a data file from a CD-ROM and zoom in to a tax parcel map and find where I lived. Mrs. D used the random point generator to locate a point to ground truth, then I had to use the map to actually locate the place that I had to ground truth.

There were some things that I didn't understand. There was some reflective data, and there was some data that we had to cluster, and I wasn't quite sure why we were doing that. But I'm amazed about how many different types of data are out there.

We went to two different stream sites. We were measuring discharge, and I was surprised that I was able to plot the information we found on a graph, so I was developing and applying new skills in ways I never imagined.

On "Growing Up Digital"

We first got a computer when I was in sixth grade and it ran on DOS. We still have it. I think since third grade, I've been exposed to computers. Basically I use it for word processing and games. We learned in school some basic programming and spreadsheets, how to program in Pascal. This past November, we got a Pentium, we got a scanner, Internet connection, Windows 95. So now I can use email and send stuff back and forth between my home and school accounts, I can use Excel, I can make charts, I can import data, I can take stuff off of disks, so then when I went into geoscience, I knew what to do. So I don't have an excessively strong background, but compared to a lot of people that I know, I know what I'm doing.

In Summary

Hearing this story from its many perspectives can help us to picture what it means to teach a capstone course devoted to original research for all involved: the teachers, the students, and the community. In her reflections on teaching and learning with GIS, Dana has shared both the triumphs and the pitfalls. Earlier in the chapter, I labeled much of her partner Hal's comments under the heading "Tolerating Ambiguity." Let's keep in mind that this is perhaps the premier high school in the nation as we consider some of the issues Dana and Hal have raised about conducting research with students and GIS.

- partnership in collaborative learning and teaching
- mirroring the uncertainties of real-world research
- unpredictability of day-to-day activities
- the freedom to learn from and with students
- modeling learning as students and teachers jointly solve problems
- integrating technology not for its own sake, but for solving the problem
- connecting with and contributing to the community

In the next chapter, we visit Canada, where one of the teachers has a different perspective on the gender issues. The close relationship with government and community agencies we've seen in the U.S. examples is relatively absent in the Canadian example. There are differences in the ways GIS has been generated and funded between the two neighbors. Accordingly, we'll see a slightly different cast to the types of activities students are involved in, but, as in the other examples we've seen, there has been a migration of GIS vertically over time and through the grade levels and laterally across curricula.

● The GIS Connection

The GIS Connection for this chapter connects you to NASA activities for students from K to 12.

9

Problem Solving in Canada

Our final visit takes us out of the U.S. and into Canada, where two geography teachers had been teaching GIS since 1994 in the context of their geographics course at the grade 10–11 level. GIS in its earliest form was developed in Canada. In the Canadian (British-style) curriculum, geography is taught as a core course at every grade level. Because of this strong value placed on geography as a core subject, Canadian teachers and schools may be able to progress more quickly on the whole integrating GIS than their counterparts in the U.S.

Jack and Dan have entirely too much fun teaching! Visiting the Star School and their classroom was refreshing. For one, it's a private boys' school, but this pair of teachers know how to have a good time and do what they do extremely well. I interviewed Jack, Dan, and six students in their classroom. Two or three geographics classes cycled through the room while I conducted the interviews off in a corner of the room. Students were working in pairs on projects ranged from finding appropriate locations for Olympics events to locating the Jewish community in the city.

In Their Own Words

In their early explorations of GIS, Jack and Dan teamed up to work together. Jack explains how he became interested, and then Dan describes how their collaboration took off.

Jack on Hearing About GIS from a Former Student

Jack: A student of mine [from my former school, Galileo High] had gone off to Ryerson Tech and he called me up one day and said, "You've got to see what they're doing up here!" So I had a couple of days, I went down and it was MapInfo version 2 and Idrisi and he starts showing me this stuff and I went, "Whoa!" Initially what I did was I brought my students down there. They built a lab and my former student Marco took the job as the lab technician and he would open the lab on Saturdays and we would take the class and go down there! The kids went nuts. So then I managed to get one computer at school, got to meet this professor.

Dan must've gotten wind of GIS somehow. Then Dan called Ryerson about GIS, and they said if you want to talk to someone talk to Jack, so he called me and we sat down in front of a machine and I showed him MapInfo and his eyes lit up and we connected. So it was like, "Yeah, we could do this and we could do this and we could do this!"

Developing a Course and Workbook

Jack: So we agreed that we could come in here and write all this down. So Dan invited me and we spent about a year and a half [working on it]. We needed a technician, so we got Angie, who was one of my former students. As a matter of fact, a lot of students from Galileo went on to Ryerson. There's a lot of job opportunities in GIS.

This [Star] school is different. You're not going to get a lot of kids from here going to Ryerson—here they're going to be doctors and lawyers. What happened here was I just said one day, "Gee, I'd love to work here." So a job opened up in the lower grades and so I dropped right in. So I took a one-year leave, a second year's leave, and now I've just had to resign [from Galileo] and now I'm here [at Star School].

Dan's Initiative

Dan: I first found out about GIS at a geography teachers' meeting and I saw some software vendors with some mapping software and saw it as an exciting way to teach geography. I didn't in the beginning have any idea. I used MapInfo first. I started to investigate GIS and found out that Ryerson has an applied geography department, so I called and spoke with them. They said, "Get a software like MapInfo and call Jack at Galileo." So I bought a few computers—this would be six years ago now.

Jack and I worked together in the evenings and arranged to hire a young woman who'd been his student to teach us and to write up some activities that we could use in our classrooms. We realized that there was a great market for a workbook, so we spent a year putting that together. So it's been five years that we've been teaching this course.

This is my ninth or tenth year here. I remember walking by the computer class and they were working on WordPerfect 5.1 and I remember arguing, "Why would you do this?" That's how far I've come in nine years!

Jack: We put a lot of hours into it. Now it's a lot of fun because we know what we're doing. What we knew in MapInfo, we had to relearn in ArcInfo— we were [saying], "How do you put a map on the screen?"

Jack on Geography in the Canadian Curriculum

As Jack explains, the Canadian curriculum is quite rich in geography, coming from the British traditional curriculum.

Jack: They have Canadian geography in ninth—human geography in eighth, in grade 7 they have physical geography, in sixth they had Canadian geography again. Six and nine are not repeated but [ninth is] more in depth. These kids have learned to think spatially. They already know what scale is, they already know what direction is—we don't have to deal with that at all because they already understand that.

The workbook [we wrote] has been tested by these guys [Star students]. One thing that's important is that if you teach GIS, you've got to teach it a second time, because the first time will be so frustrating, and if you can work together with the kids at first, then the second time around, you can be a little more detached and say, "Yeah, I know the problem you're facing." Then you look like a real pro! Or you sit down and say, "What do you think? What do you think your next step is?"

On Pedagogical Issues of GIS in Education

Because Jack and Dan have been teaching this course over a period of years, they've had time to reflect on some of the nuances of student learning, and, as Dana raised, the pedagogical issues. As they learned, they taught one another how to use MapInfo, a different GIS software used primarily by commercial industry. Jack and Dan decided to coauthor the workbook, but made a switch midstream to ESRI's ArcView. Again, ESRI had taken more of a lead in developing K–12 support for GIS in education. Back in 1997, I used their workbook to teach a course in GIS. It's a workbook with a sense of humor. How (regrettably) uncommon is that?

Dan comments on the workbook and how students respond to it.

Dan: Our workbook is written in a very linear fashion, which is the way that I learned to use the software. We tried to write with our sense of humor so that it's appropriate for kids. I think they found it almost too—the baby steps—the first part of each activity is primarily the baby steps, going from A to B to C to D. They would rather go from A to D—the hell with B and C—we'll get there, you know? They just sort of make these big jumps. Kids are really adept at the software. They tend to be intuitive.

On "Growing Up Digital"

Jack: The kids' computer skills are extremely high. The majority of them are scary in what they know. And that's the other thing—the teacher teaching this course has to be humble and accept the fact that you have to say to the kids, "Show me?" That's important. Jason is one of those kids. A lot of times I'll say, "Jason?"—not for GIS, but for files, saving data—they know all the tricks.

Three years ago at Galileo, the kids didn't have computers at home, but they didn't take long. Here [at Star] they *do* come from homes with computers. These guys are on the computers almost from the first day.

On Gender Issues in GIS

Jack: If there's any [gender] difference, I think girls are better working independently. What I found is a lot of the girls were working independently much better. If you put two girls together in front of a computer, they'll work. Two guys will hit each other, smash each other. Other than that, Angie [our Galileo student who became our technical assistant] is a good example.

A Pedagogy of Facilitation, Co-construction, and Co-instruction

The easygoing pace and the humility with which these teachers describe their work in part belies their own long hours preparing to teach the course by creating the workbook. Yet they readily admit the different role the GIS instructor must take. It seems inherent in GIS—there are so many ways to approach and solve problems that it engenders co-construction and co-instruction—we've heard that from several teachers. These two actually seem to enjoy it! Again, working collaboratively as a team is central.

Both Dan and Jack see some of the critical issues of learning and teaching with GIS as becoming more integrated through a problem-solving approach.

Jack: There are so many different ways of solving the problems. I'll give you a good example. I gave them a test a week ago. A bomb was going to explode in another part of Ontario because we have data on Ontario, and I wanted them to figure out how many people had to be evacuated. And I solved it doing it one way. And during the test, four kids figured out four other ways of doing it! Then I realized there are five ways of figuring out the same question! And then one kid figured out that I'd made a mistake! We analyzed it and what I did in the end is that every kid got a 10 out of 10 because each boy found a solution, so it became not a test, but a graded assignment.

Dan: It's the notion of solving problems and incorporating into it what's really important in education, and that's critical thinking skills. You sometimes lose sight of that in education when you get bogged down with how to manipulate the software. We're teaching kids how to think—how to think creatively, how to think independently, how to solve problems. Really, GIS is just another tool, like a pen, and if it's not, then what're we doing with it?

There's some kids right now doing a study of the Jewish neighborhood here in the city. It's very superficial—there's no profound thing here, but they're just essentially trying to define it and look at the history of it. So now I've asked them to go to other resources like the Internet to find other features of the Jewish community. One of the things I've found is that our students are very poor at finding information from the Internet. They think it's all there, but they don't know how to find information. If they'd made a phone call, they could've gotten the information a lot quicker!

In the workplace, GIS solutions are shared among the technicians using it. Therefore, the teaching and learning of GIS in many ways reflects the landscape of the workplace. I've called these "new landscapes of learning with technology," and in many ways that is how technology alters the work and educational landscapes.

Jack: A lot of [the students] like independent work; *like* that they're given a problem to solve. A lot of them really love the presentation, the layout of the maps; *like* that after you've done the map, you use [it in] the Corel or PowerPoint presentation.

What I'd really love to see is like history and science starting to use it, maybe bring up historical data. Remote sensing is a great way to integrate the historic information. I'd love to have a kid in *any* class saying, "I could use GIS for this." It's so endless what these guys can do—you get on the Internet and you see what schools are doing with it on the rivers and this kind of thing.

The GIS Connection

The GIS Connection for this chapter is an activity that builds on this concept of mapping ethnicity. One example is the Chinese immigration project by Chialing Lai, on the companion CD. We also suggest how to mine community resources such as—as Dan mentions—the telephone book and other resources.

Community Partnership

Even with all of their expertise, Jack and Dan have community and industry partners. Initially, this was especially important since in Canada, there are greater restrictions on data availability than in the U.S. Because of the early development of GIS by specific parties, not by the government per se, GIS data was generated in a more proprietary way, and therefore wasn't freely exchanged, and in fact, was often prohibitively expensive for a school budget.

Jack: Ryerson and ESRI are now where we get our technical aid, and they're our closest partners. A lot of levels of government that I spoke to have been helpful with discounting prices because we're educational. Or as soon as they hear—you'll get these guys on the phone that say, "Oh, you're at a high school? This is great! This is where it should be!" and they're very helpful that way. Some of the data they will let you have, like when you tell them that you're a school, they'll say, "Okay, fine, as long as you use it for educational purposes," but it's very limited.

But ESRI has done a good job of creating an ArcCanada CD with Canadian data on it and it's expanding, so eventually the government is getting it through their heads that this stuff has to go to the schools. But they're all surprised that we're doing it in high school. Even in the States, talking to people, it's the same thing. Eventually I'd like to see more cooperative work to develop some of these things. There are some other teachers at the public schools who are catching up.

Dan: We work with ESRI. Other people tend to work with us. [Star] is really the senior partner. People call us from other schools. We sell the workbook to help people incorporate GIS into the classroom.

Toward Community Service Learning

Perhaps because of the more proprietary nature of GIS information in Canada, the local government connections hadn't developed in the ways they have in the U.S. schools, but Jack clearly sees the value of having students perform GIS problem solving for the community. Recall DaVinci teacher Hal's caveat that the students not be exploited in performing the service, but be *learning* through service. This caveat is, of course central to Community Service Learning (CSL) theory.

Jack: Next year we're planning to build a lab. By the time they get to the geographics course, they're going to say, "Sir, we've already had all this." The future of this course is more connection to the Internet, remote sensing. GPS is the next stage as well. And, this is interesting. As the knowledge of GIS filters down the grades, the nature of this course and the activities will have to change because they'll already know them. Less teaching *about* GIS but more solving problems *using* GIS. That's what we're stressing.

Wouldn't it be great if a school like this could offer its GIS and services training others? It's connected to the real world, and this is a real-world problem and we can help to solve it for them. I can see it working in a small community easier—"Would you like us to help you?"

[In the future], I see GIS incorporated in all subjects at all levels. With the Internet and this onslaught of data? This is a great way to bring it all together. What I would love to do is talk to the faculties of education and expose them to GIS and have the new teachers have an understanding of GIS. That would be great.

Teacher Training with Students as Teaching Assistants

Jack and Dan had initiated teacher training workshops. Unquestionably leaders in the field, the two also work with Ryerson Technical College as faculty in a certificate program for teachers in geotechnology. (See <www.geography.ryerson.ca/newhtml/geotech.htm>.) Keep in mind that in Canada, many teachers will already possess a bachelor's degree in geography, so these courses can begin from that assumption. As perhaps the first program of its kind, the Ryerson model has become a *de facto* model for such programs internationally.

Jack: Last year it was a four-day, this year it's a five-day teacher training. This year we're doing it in two stages. Our ESRI partner is going to do an advanced course because there are actually some people who are ready for that, and we're going to do the beginners in GIS. We're also going to do a training at a school near here at a technology event for their geography component. We were talking about having [K–12] students come in and help teach the teacher training course because they could actually teach better than we could.

Dan and Jack were among the first to ask students to be part of their instructional team, and in subsequent teacher workshops, have employed students as teaching assistants. We borrowed this practice for our GIS in Education course and the participant response to the student TA was very positive.

In Summary

Dan has elucidated an important point about teaching with any technology—that for him, the real issue is teaching the critical thinking skills, and using appropriate instructional technologies to serve those overarching educational goals. The pair's focus on problem solving was evident from the student interviews. To a man, each and every Star student interviewee described GIS as a tool for problem solving. They had internalized the value of GIS for a purpose. While I did hear this from one or two students in each of the other schools, I was struck by the fact that at Star, all of the boys had internalized this view.

Because this course is part of a core geography curriculum, its curricular scope is delineated by national and provincial guidelines. Dan and Jack had worked closely with their provincial organization to align the geographics course with the curricular goals (posted at <www.esricanada.com>). Needless to say, these are more highly defined in Canada than in the U.S. The closest comparable U.S. guidelines are found in the "Geography for Life" standards developed by the National Council for Geographic Education and others (available at <www.ncge.org>).

10

Conclusions and Implications

With our examples from eastern North America, given that the data were gathered in 1998–99, there are several common features and many illuminating implications for not just GIS in social studies, but also for conducting social studies, for reconsidering social studies scope and sequence, and for transforming social studies through community partnership, interdisciplinary collaboration, and technology integration.

In order to discuss this, I've called upon my critical self—the teacher of twenty-odd years who's seen different educational fads and fashions come and go. I've weighed the research and writing of this book against that critical educator—as those who know me can well attest. I constantly question whether what I'm doing is worth it. Sure, I'm a reflective practitioner, but I'm also realistic, pragmatic, and have major concerns about the two primary resources:time and energy.

So I've asked my critical side to pose the questions I think need to be addressed in terms of whether in social studies we should consider integrating this technology. I've raised some of the critical issues around the technology itself in Chapter 7, so we won't revisit those, but what about the pedagogical issues? Let's pose the null hypothesis first.

What If We *Don't* Integrate GIS into Social Studies?

Essentially, we know how the social studies curriculum will continue to be conceived. In general, according to O. L. Davis, it really hasn't changed since its basic conception in the early 1900s. What's changed somewhat is an awareness of thematic possibilities, but the overwhelming content of U.S.

history, world cultures and civilizations, economics, geography, and the behavioral sciences is enough to choke a horse and provide trivia questions for both games and standardized tests for all eternity.

So if we don't decide to conduct social studies, with or without GIS, what we'd miss is an opportunity to connect with the community over real issues, develop mutual capacity with other institutions and agencies, and have the chance to delve with students into real inquiry in social studies curricula.

Who Needs Critical Thinking and Problem Solving?

All teachers have seen students blindly following fashion and consumerism in place of authentic self-development and self-actualization. The crime of material substitution for Maslow's hierarchy of needs cries out to social studies to lead students toward critical thinking and problem solving. Through using GIS, students came to a critical understanding of the limitations of *data*. This understanding needs to be part of a broader critique of all media. Critical thinking is a threat to those who wish to control by other than moral authority or integrity. The critical issues inherent in the Science, Technology, and Society theme should be our call in social studies.

Through the joint problem solving so evident in all of these schools, students are learning what they need to be responsible adults who can make decisions not simply based on "what is given," but from developed skills and habits of looking at what is behind the *data*. These are the types of skills and habits of mind we need to develop in our students in order to feel confident in their abilities to create a world of sustainable communities.

From construction trades to historic preservationists, who doesn't need to understand spatial concepts and problems? To a prospective health care worker or doctor, how would *not* understanding the relationship between locations and conditions of population, disease, and environmental features affect the community's public health?

I found it utterly energizing throughout this research process to be among educators who were concerned about critical thinking and issues even as they were in the throes of developing ways to learn and research themselves *as they were teaching*. Yes—that's the joy—the joy we've forgotten to exalt—usually those who teach are those who love to learn! But it's easy to become lulled by content into habits of pure "cultural transmission" without the mission—the mission of learning and social construction of the world we want, learning as we teach, with students. It's a matter of energy. My mentor, Seth Kreisberg (1992), called it "power-with" students. It's basically mutually enhanced power or energy shared between teachers and students.

The joy I heard each of the interviewed teachers describe when asking their students how to execute this or that—"How can we do this?" "How are you going to approach this?" "What do we need to do next?"—can't possibly be replaced by simple content transmission. In authentic community problem solving, when the students "get it," it's truly theirs *and* the community's—they become reconnected in a way that no isolated content can connect them.

What Will Be the Future Context of Geography in Social Studies?

As we move forward into this century, we'll see our concepts of political spaces and systems tested and retested. The impacts of 9/11/2001; the euro; rebuilding Afghanistan—how? The Chinese Olympics in 2008 will signal a huge transition globally. The centrality of geography in the social studies curriculum can no longer be ignored in the U.S. or elsewhere, and Canada's lead should be our model.

As a context for integrating one of the most ubiquitous technologies on the planet—and off the planet as well—GIS has staying power in a terms of the skill set twenty-first century students will use. As a conceptual and instructional technology it is extremely potent and should exert a greater demand for geography in the curriculum.

Capstone Courses in Social Studies?

Looking across the projects and courses represented in the book, the possibility of capstone courses in secondary social studies is tremendously appealing. Light-years beyond the history report, this authentic concentrated inquiry would be a preparation for any student heading into almost any conceivable field.

Where and How Do We Integrate Community Service Learning?

How original research benefits the community has, I hope, been demonstrated in Chapters 3 through 9—this is beyond serving soup (which is very important)—and connects students to the *future* of their communities. Several of these projects have had an impact beyond their own communities as well. "*Why* are there homeless people needing food?" is the question *behind* "How can I help feed the homeless?"

The capstone course offers a brilliant option for where and how we might integrate GIS and conducting social studies, as modeled by one of the nation's foremost high schools. Many schools require only three years of social studies. Here is a way to connect and conduct social studies with technology or other courses in original research opportunities. This also represents a model for the future of our own multidiscipline.

The importance of students' connections to humanity and to the planet are increasingly critical in grounding their values and understandings in order to address increasingly complex problems. With content courses behind them, seniors in social studies could exercise original research, perform community service, and become part of the effort toward sustainable communities.

Incorporating a Constructivist Pedagogy of Inquiry

How will the social studies teachers of the future be able to incorporate this style of teaching and learning? A constructivist pedagogy based upon skill development can facilitate inquiry learning and teaching. Assessing what kinds of skills students have as resources is a completely different tack than starting blindly into a text-dependent course with no true "final product."

When teachers fear the consequences of poor test scores, their inclinations to innovate are severely affected, morale is low, and "constructivism" sounds suspiciously like making things up on the fly. Abandoning the comfort of content in order to develop skills, integrate new technologies, take chances—invent a capstone course? Are we joking? The answer is, No! Recalling the advantages given to those "academically gifted" or magnet school students, we must recommit to providing equitable learning opportunities for all students. While it feels counterintuitive, like countersocialization, or counter–mandated testing, it is possible, necessary, and it produces results.

Now, as ever, it is the teacher's responsibility to make the micropolitical choices that will either simply reconstitute the past or will begin to constitute the future. In each classroom, the increments of change that are ignited by simply asking, "How can we do this?" "Who knows how to show us that software?" "Who among you could co-teach your classmates?" Using "power-with" students is the way we reshape the curriculum and the community. The learning benefits are those that empower students to discipline themselves, their own minds, and their communities.

Why Take Up Co-constructivist Practice?

Asking students to come to the tasks of original inquiry with what technology skills they may have—asking them to co-instruct and co-construct—was evident in every one of these projects. As I honestly reflect on my practice of integrating technology at the secondary, undergraduate, and graduate levels, I can't claim to have done it by myself! The students have always been part of the equation—helping one another or showing one another (and their teacher!) tricks, shortcuts, functions, and entire software applications. The point is, that's a good thing, because the teacher is still leading through *modeling learning* with students.

Social studies teachers have had to come to grips with the fact that they can never know all of history, all of geography, all of any of the subfields. We must accept that ambiguity is part of the mastery of teaching; it is the informed and mature guiding and leading that become more salient as teachers become experienced. It is even more essential that experienced teachers reconnect with the joy of *learning* in order to stay intellectually alive and well!

Co-constructivist practice means incorporating resources from a variety of locations and becoming the conduit for learning. When students are given the responsibility to perform as adults (which has become an invisible goal of education), they perform responsibly. It is what they most need and want to do. It is the wisdom of practice that allows teachers to lead and use their own and the energy of students wisely.

Do I Really Have to Open the Door to Interdisciplinary Collaboration?

The opening to co-constructivist teaching and learning makes more possible the teaming in which I strongly recommend GIS integration take place. In our GIS in Education graduate course, we are focusing on work with instructional technology master's candidates to support integration of GIS across disciplines. Most have developed social studies projects, many in collaboration with fellow teachers. Because, as I will expand upon below, GIS is a relatively dialogic application—the sharing of data as an almost built-in expectation on collaboration—GIS is best done as a collaborative problem-solving endeavor and with partners. The mutual benefits and capacity building have been amply described.

Is It Really Okay to Engage Students as Agents and Assistants?

If it takes time to develop collaborative relationships with teaching colleagues, in the meanwhile, any of the many programs in which students act as technical assistants, teaching assistants, community service liaisons, or agents at large mandates utilizing that resource: young people! This new phenomenon of educational-sociology is one of the best innovations to have emerged in the last decade. What a wonderful resource I found when I visited Rebecca's classroom and had an assistant ready and waiting to assist the teacher and the class! Think about Zach in his early adoption of ArcView without a manual. Recall Dana's mentorship student who continued to be a liaison to USGS for the geosystems class and Jack's former student who introduced him—and now, so many other Canadian teachers—to GIS.

Naturally, there is a balance that must be struck in reconsidering students' roles as active participants. As an advisor for the newspaper and yearbook for ten years, I was used to giving students responsibility. I depended on students—I had to—and because I did, and because they wanted to respond responsibly, I'm relieved to say that in those ten years I only encountered one violation (of plagiarism). I attribute that relatively sound record to the fact that students *want* to be treated as responsible citizens. I fear that if we as social studies teachers don't create those conditions, then we aren't addressing a major part of our mission.

How Will Education on the Whole Be Different?

I believe—even as the testing and textbook industries detest the thought—that the emergent landscapes of learning will look more like those described by these pioneers. They are looking at the "new world" of learning and teaching. While textbooks may never become completely obsolete, they will become relegated to their proper magnitude as resources for teaching and learning, alongside the newer resources that are emerging—the Internet, new resources on DVD, and other sources—and not just media, but the real connections students will be able to make with other students, researchers, and "experts."

When the social studies can combine *actual* field-based learning, *virtual* applications, the use of *critical* thinking, and the exercising of *ethical* problem solving and decision making, we will have made progress toward the mission of social studies.

How and Where Does GIS Fit into the New Landscapes of Learning?

These new landscapes of learning reflect the workplaces and spaces as transformed by the new communications media. As usual, schools will follow—not lead—the trend, but the central role and *function* of school in the community should become revitalized. What schools shouldn't do is become inflexibly locked in an unchanging model. It is, I think, a resurgence of the role of the school as a beacon of service to the community as conduits toward new synergies of society, of place, of diversity, and of equity.

Technical Assistance: The Nature of GIS Is That No One Knows It All

It is therefore important to understand the nature of GIS and how it fosters collaboration—in data gathering, in data generation, sharing, and problem solving. There is no one person or entity that possesses all of the GIS information! It is a networked system of publicly and privately maintained data, representations, and information. In the U.S., the citizens have paid for much of the system's components—the satellites that generate the imagery, the census information that is gathered, the geographic, atmospheric, and transportation networks that constitute it. As such, those who work in public, government, or other agencies with this data have, as part of their mission, a return of the information to its citizen underwriters. I have found GIS agents and technicians committed to public education at every turn and in every part of the continent.

As well, the private developers such as ESRI and other GIS software purveyors have been forthcoming in educational initiatives and enterprises. Technical assistants are another good thing for teachers. Like us, they are public servants and can assist in projects and applications. They're just an email away—ESRI "folks," as they call themselves, local town, city, or county GIS agents—they're out there and they are willing to assist you. See the companion CD for ways to connect to them!

How Can the Generation "Growing Up Digital" Connect Schools and Communities with GIS?

Finally, when students become connected to their communities—both in the actual and the virtual domains—we have begun to transform both school and community, bringing them back together as joint locations of living and learning. With their skills already awaiting a real application—not just a computer game or simulation—students can begin to realize their own place and potential as contributing members of the community. When I consider their energy, their potential, and their commitment to the future of our communities and our planet, I shudder to think what we could lose if we miss the opportunity.

With that, we hope to hear from you, to begin to connect you to a growing web of committed educators, and we hope you will enjoy exploring the CD, the Internet, your community's GIS resources, and the various pathways we've illuminated toward the new landscapes of learning and teaching.

References

Alibrandi, Marsha, Candy Beal, Anna Wilson, Rita Hagevik, Betty Mackie, Virginia Owens, Neville Sinclair, and Ann Thompson. 2001. "Students Reclaim Their Community's History: Interdisciplinary Research with Technological Applications." In *Teaching Together: Improving Social Studies Teaching and Learning Through School/University Collaboration*, edited by Christenson, Johnson, and Norris. Washington, DC: National Council for Social Studies.

Alibrandi, Marsha. 1998. "GIS as a Tool in Environmental Studies: Student, Teacher, and Community Perspectives." *Meridian* (June). Accessed at <http://www2.ncsu.edu/unity/lockers/project/meridian/jun98/feat2-3/feat2-3.html>.

———. 1997. "Thinking Spatially: GIS in the High School Classroom." *Green Teacher* 50.

———. 1993. Mental Maps: Understanding Spatial Cognition Through Artifacts. Unpublished qualifying paper for comprehensive examination, University of Massachusetts, Amherst, MA.

Berry, Wendell. 2002. *In the Presence of Fear: Three Essays for a Changed World*. North Adams, MA: Orion Society.

Butchart, Ronald. 1986. *Local Schools: Exploring Their History*. (*Nearby History* series.) Walnut Creek, CA: AltaMira Press.

Davis, O. L., and Howard D. Mehinger, eds. 1981. *The Social Studies: Eightieth Yearbook of the National Society for the Study of Education*. Chicago: University of Chicago Press.

Dede, Christopher. 2000. "A New Century Demands New Ways of Learning." In *The Digital Classroom*, edited by David T. Gordon. Cambridge, MA: Harvard Education Letter. Also accessible at Harvard Graduate School of Education: <www.gse.harvard.edu/news/features/dc_dede12012000.html>.

Downs, Roger, and David Stea. 1977. *Maps in Minds*. New York: Harper & Row.

Erickson, Frederick. 1984. "School Literacy, Reasoning and Civility: An Anthropological Perspective." *Review of Educational Research* 54 (4): 525–546.

Freire, Paolo. [1968] 1988. *Pedagogy of the Oppressed.* New York: Continuum.

Gardner, Howard. 1983. *Frames of Mind: The Theory of Multiple Intelligences.* New York: Basic.

Geographic Education National Implementation Project (GENIP). 1987. *7–12 Geography Themes, Key Ideas, and Learning Opportunities.* Indiana, PA: National Council for Geographic Education.

Golledge, Reginald G., and Robert J. Stimson. 1996. *Spatial Behavior.* New York: Guilford Press.

Hall, Edward T. 1966. *The Hidden Dimension.* Garden City, NY: Doubleday.

Haque, Akhlaque. 2001. "GIS, Public Service, and the Issue of Democratic Governance." *Public Administration Review* 61 (3): 259–263.

Harley, J. B. 1990. "Cartography, Ethics, and Social Theory." *Cartographica* 27 (1): 1–23.

Harr, Robert. 1995. *A Civil Action.* New York: Random House.

Hartoonian, H. Michael. 1996. The Price of Civilization: Competence and Constant Vigil. Presidential address delivered at the 75th Annual Conference of the National Council for the Social Studies, Chicago, IL. Reprinted in *Social Education* (January): 6–8.

Kelley, Kevin. 1988. *The Home Planet.* Reading, MA: Addison-Wesley.

Kemmis, Daniel. 1990. *Community and the Politics of Place.* Normal, OK: University of Oklahoma Press.

Klein, Marylin, and David P. Fogle. 1990. *Clues to American Architecture.* River City Publishing.

Kreisberg, Seth. 1992. *Transforming Power: Domination, Empowerment, and Education.* Albany: State University of New York Press.

Lakoff, George, and Mark Johnson. 1980. *Metaphors We Live By.* Chicago: University of Chicago Press.

Least Heat Moon, William. 1991. *PrairyErth (A Deep Map): An Epic History of the Tallgrass Prairie Country.* Boston: Houghton Mifflin.

Liben, Lynn. 1995. "Educational Applications of GIS: A Developmental Psychologist's Perspective." *The EdGIS Conference Report*, NSF95-124. Cambridge, MA: TERC.

Liben, Lynn, Anne Patterson, and Nora Newcombe. 1981. *Spatial Representation and Behavior Across the Lifespan.* New York: Academic.

Lynch, Kevin. 1960. *Image of the City.* Cambridge, MA: MIT Press.

MacAulay, David. 1983. *City: A Story of Roman Planning and Construction.* Boston: Houghton Mifflin.

MacAulay, David. 1983. *Underground.* Boston: Houghton Mifflin.

Maslow, Abraham, Robert Frager, and James Fadiman. 1987. *Motivation and Personality.* 3d ed. Boston: Addison-Wesley.

McBride, James. 1996. *The Color of Water: A Black Man's Tribute to His White Mother.* New York: Putnam.

Monmonier, Mark. 1991. *How to Lie with Maps.* Chicago: University of Chicago Press.

Nietschmann, Bernard. 1987. "The Third World War." *Cultural Survival Quarterly* 11 (3): 1–16.

O'Looney, John. 2000. *Beyond Maps: GIS Decision Making in Local Government.* Redlands, CA: ESRI.

Percoco, James. 1998. *A Passion for the Past: Creative Teaching of United States History.* Portsmouth, NH: Heinemann.

Pickles, John. 1995. *Ground Truth: Social Implications of GIS.* New York: Guilford Press.

Pinker, Steven. 1994. *The Language Instinct.* New York: William Morrow and Co.

Postel, Sandra, and Linda Starke, eds. 1997. *Last Oasis: Facing Water Scarcity.* 2d ed. New York: W.W. Norton.

Saarinen, Thomas. 1988. *Environmental Planning, Perception, and Behavior.* Prospect Heights, IL: Waveland Press.

Sarnoff, Herschel. 2002. "Census 1790: A GIS Project." *Teaching to Change LA: The Digital Divide, Vol. 1 No. 2.* UCLA: Institute for Democracy, Education and Access. Accessed at <www.tcla.gseis.ucla.edu/divide /teachers/lausd_jordan.html> (6 March 2002).

Sizer, Theodore. 1992. *Horace's School: Redesigning the American High School.* Boston: Houghton Mifflin.

Snyder, Gary. 1995. *A Place in Space: Ethics, Aesthetics and Watersheds.* Washington, DC: Counterpoint Press.

Snyder, Will, and Marsha Alibrandi. 2002. Earth Connection Roundtables: A Resource for High School Networking. Paper presented at the Annual Conference of the North American Association for Environmental Education, Boston, MA.

Sobel, Dava. 1996. *Longitude: The True Story of a Lone Genius Who Solved the Greatest Scientific Problem of His Time.* New York: Penguin.

Sobel, David. 1998. *Mapmaking with Children: Sense of Place Education for the Elementary Years.* Portsmouth, NH: Heinemann.

———. 1997. "Take Back the Afternoon: Preserving the Landscape of Childhood in Spite of Computers." Accessed at <http://csf.colorado .edu/sine/internet/sobel.html>.

———. 1996. *Beyond Ecophobia: Reclaiming the Heart in Nature Education.* Northampton, MA: Orion Society.

Tapscott, Donald. 1998. *Growing Up Digital.* New York: McGraw-Hill.

Theobald, Paul. 1997. *Teaching the Commons: Place, Pride, and the Renewal of Community*. Boulder, CO: Westview Press.

Tolman, E. 1948. *Behavior and Psychological Man: Essays in Motivation and Learning*. Berkeley, CA: University of California Press.

Tuan, Yi- Fu. 1977. *Space and Place: The Perspective of Experience*. Minneapolis: University of Minnesota Press.

Vosniadou, Stella, and William Brewer. 1992. "Mental Models of the Earth." *Cognitive Psychology* 24: 535–585.

Williams-Vinson, Ella Arrington. 1996. *Both Sides of the Tracks: A Profile of the Colored Community, Cary, North Carolina*. Cary, NC: Author.

Wilson, Edward O. 1992. *The Diversity of Life*. Cambridge, MA: Harvard University Press.

Wilson, Edward O., ed. 1989. *Biodiversity*. Washington, DC: National Academy Press.

Winston, Barbara. 1989. On Geography and Global Education. Lecture presented at the Summer Geographic Institute, Washington, DC.

Yolen, Jane. 1995. *Letting Swift River Go*. Boston: Little, Brown.

Resources

Chapter 1

GIS Jobs Clearinghouse:
National Council for the Social Studies (NCSS):
    <www.ncss.org/standards/exec.html>

Chapter 3

ESRI's Community Atlas Project: <www.esri.com/communityatlas>
ESRI EdUC (Educator's User Conference: <www.esri.com/gisedconf>
ESRI's School GIS website: <www.esri.com/k-12>
ESRI's ArcLessons website: <www.esri.com/arclessons>
Sarnoff's "Census 1790: Slaves as Percent of US Population in each State"
    project is available on the Web at:
        <www.tcla.gseis.ucla.edu/divide/teachers/lausd_jordan.html>

Chapter 8

Anderson Classification System: Land use categories determined by satellite
    imaging: <www.geography.wisc.edu/sco/maps/landcover.html>

Chapter 9

Ryerson Tech GIS program:
    <www.geography.ryerson.ca./newhtml/geotech.htm>
National Council of Geographic Education: <www.ncge.org>

Additional References and Resources for Teachers

GISinEducation website is our own website housed at North Carolina State
    University's College of Education. Shannon White, codesigner of the

GISC activities, is the webmaster. Please visit the site for links to useful resources! <www.ncsu.edu/gisined>

GIS Connections to community geographic information providers, accessed at <http://clearinghouse1.fgdc.gov/registry/clearinghouse_sites.html>

Heinemann, accessed at <www.heinemann.com>

Kerski, Joseph. 2000. The Implementation and Effectiveness of Geographic Information Systems Technology and Method in Secondary Education. Ph.D. dissertation, University of Colorado.

Knowles, Anne Kelly, ed. 2002. *Past Time, Past Place: GIS for History*. Redlands, CS: ESRI Press.

Malone, Lyn, Anita Palmer, and Christine Voigt. 2002. *Mapping Our World: GIS Lessons for Educators*. Redlands, CA: ESRI Press.

———. 2002. *Community Geography: GIS in Action, Teacher's Guide*. Redlands, CA: ESRI Press.

Mapping America's Battlefields Project (American Battlefield Protection Program, Heritage Preservation Services, National Park Service)· <www2.cr.nps.gov/gis/battlefield.htm>

Massachusetts Water Resources Authority curricula: <www.madwep.org/education_teachers.htm>

Orton Family Foundation. *Community Mapping Program:* <www.orton.org/community_mapping>

Thompson, Ann, and Rita Hagevik. 1999. *Satellites, Computers, and Mapping*. Syllabus and student projects: <www.ncsu.edu/midlink/gis/courseoutline.htm>

Zanelli English, Kim, and Laura S. Feaster. 2002. *Community Geography: GIS in Action*. Redlands, CA: ESRI Press.